The Holy Spirit: Believer's Guide

Herschel H. Hobbs

The Holy Spirit

Believer's Guide

BROADMAN PRESS
NASHVILLE, TENNESSEE

To
HIM
whom to glorify is the
role of the Holy Spirit

Preface

Our generation is witnessing a revival of interest in the person and work of the Holy Spirit. This revival centers not in the various Pentecostal movements but in many of the older, more established Christian bodies. Unfortunately, however, in such a revival there is always the danger that interest will center in the more ecstatic elements to the neglect of the basic ones as taught in the Scriptures. At no point in the Christian revelation is caution needed more than in matters pertaining to the Holy Spirit. The admonition of 1 John 4:1 to discern the spirits, to know whether they be of God, is still needed.

Unfortunately there is a paucity of literature dealing with the Holy Spirit as such. This may be due to a natural reaction against extremism in some quarters. It may be due to the fact that it is not easy to write such a work. Or it may be in keeping with the Holy Spirit's purpose to glorify Jesus rather than to point to himself.

However, he would not have us to be entirely ignorant concerning him. Jesus taught about him. The writers of the Scriptures portrayed him in his work. This volume is the effort of one man to set forth in part what he believes the Scriptures teach concerning the Holy Spirit. The scope of this subject prohibits an exhaustive treatment but hopefully herein are presented some helpful guidelines.

Through the years one becomes debtor to many people in the

field of ideas. Many things reflected in this work came from many people. Where possible due credit is given.

The basic English biblical text followed in this volume is the King James Version. At times we have indicated reliance upon other translations. When it seemed advisable, we have made our own translations from Nestle's *Novum Testamentum Graece,* or his version of the Greek New Testament.

Quite obviously not every reader will agree entirely with the author's interpretation of this vital subject. But if this volume helps one such reader to a better understanding, if it stimulates him to make a deeper study of the Holy Spirit, then it will in part have accomplished its mission. It is with a prayer to this end that it is sent forth.

CONTENTS

Who He Is

1

G. Henton Davies, principal of Regents Park College, Oxford University, reminds us that "our experience of the Holy Spirit is our experience of God in the 'gap.' " [1] The distinct personalities of God and man imply a gap between them. The progressive revelation of God portrays his purpose to cross that gap. In Eden and at Sinai, God visited with his people. But it was always with God on one side of the gap and man on the other side. In the Old Testament, God as the angel of the Lord appeared to men and the Spirit of the Lord worked through and upon men. But the gap was still there.

Eventually, in Jesus Christ, God himself crossed the gap as "the Word was made flesh, and dwelt among us" (John 1:14). Finally, the gap was removed completely. Following the ascension of Jesus, God in the Holy Spirit came in a special way to dwell both *with* and *within* his redeemed people (John 14:17). This last thought emphasizes the importance of an understanding of the person and work of the Holy Spirit.

Any effort to comprehend the Holy Spirit must begin with the consideration of who he is and then proceed to an examination of what he does.

In order to understand who the Holy Spirit is it is necessary to define the terms involved. Basically the name is *Spirit*. The qualifying adjective "holy" came to be associated with the name.

The English word "spirit" comes from the Latin word *spiritus*. But it is used in the Old Testament to translate the Hebrew word *ruach;* in the New Testament it renders the Greek word *pneuma* (note our word "pneumatic"). Originally, both of these biblical words meant "breath"; later they came to mean "wind" or "air"; and, finally, "spirit."

According to one Hebrew concordance the word *ruach* appears in the Old Testament about 370 times. Smith's *Greek-English Concordance* lists *pneuma* as appearing in the New Testament 385 times, 244 of these referring to the Holy Spirit. Unfortunately, in the New Testament *pneuma,* when referring to the Holy Spirit, is often rendered "Ghost" (KJV).

In both the Old and the New Testaments the Hebrew and Greek words for holy have the root meaning of separation, set apart, or dedicated to the service of a god or God. Originally they carried no moral content, even referring to immoral men and women, used in the worship of the gods and goddesses of fertility. The moral concept of righteousness came to be applied when the words were associated with Jehovah. Even so, the basic connotation of separation or dedication to Jehovah remained. Various forms of these words are also rendered "saint." It is of interest to note that whereas in the Old Testament the word "holy" more often refers to things, in the New Testament its greater emphasis is with regard to people.

Now what is the significance of these terms with reference to the Holy Spirit? Language is a living thing. It developed among men in their efforts to express life as they experienced and understood it. For instance, man noted that breath was associated with life. If a man breathed he lived; if he stopped breathing he died. So breath was associated with the invisible force of life. Furthermore, it expressed the intangible element of man's nature, hence his *spirit* or the driving force within him.

Furthermore, man was familiar with the wind. Whether it was experienced as a gentle breeze or a roaring hurricane, he knew it as a basic, invisible force in nature. So it represented power, a power for blessings or destruction according to how one related himself to it.

God reveals himself to man in terms of man's understanding. Thus as invisible power and presence he revealed himself as *ruach* or *pneuma*. For God is spirit. As "breath" he is the source of man's life, both animal, moral, and spiritual. He is the divine driving force both upon, in, and through man. God's spirit indwells man's spirit so that man in his basic nature was created in the likeness of God. It is through God's spirit that fallen man through Christ may become a child of God.

As "wind" God is the invisible, divine power at work in the universe. Man's relation to the Spirit determines whether his power shall be for good or for bad. Jesus drew upon this dual nature of *pneuma* to illustrate how this invisible but powerful presence of God works for man's good. "The wind [*pneuma*] bloweth where it listeth, and thou hearest the sound thereof, but canst not tell whence it cometh, and whither it goeth: so is every one that is born of the Spirit [*pneuma*]" (John 3:8). You cannot see the *pneuma* of God, either natural or spiritual; but you can see and experience the results of both.

And because the Spirit is the spirit of God, he is *holy* as God is holy. Therefore, he is the Holy Spirit.

A Person

God is a person. And since the Holy Spirit is the spirit of God, he also is a person. The same may be said as to the Spirit's relation to Jesus Christ. This does not mean that the Spirit is distinct and apart from God. He is deity himself in a peculiar revelation. This matter will be discussed more fully when we come to the problem of the Trinity. It should be noted, however, that while the personality of the Holy Spirit is evident in the Old Testament, it is more clearly seen in the New Testament.

The personality of the Holy Spirit may be noted under two considerations.

First, the personality of the Holy Spirit is seen in the pronouns used with reference to him. The word *pneuma* itself is a neuter form. Quite naturally, therefore, any pronoun which has *pneuma* as its immediate antecedent must also be neuter. However, since rules of grammar demand this, such can have no bearing on the question of the personality of the Holy Spirit. It is significant, however, that all pronouns referring to the Holy Spirit, but which do not have *pneuma* as their immediate antecedent, are masculine in form.

For instance, John 14:26 reads, "The Comforter, which is the Holy Ghost, whom [*ho,* masculine] the Father will send in my name, he [*ekeinos,* masculine] shall teach you all things." Likewise, John 15:26, "The Spirit of truth, which [*ho*] proceedeth from the Father, he [*ekeinos*] shall testify of me." The personality of the Holy Spirit is emphasized in John 16:13. Here *ekeinos* (masculine) is in apposition with "the Spirit of truth" (*to pneuma tēs alētheias,* neuter). "He [masculine], the Spirit of truth" [neuter].

The masculine pronoun gives personality to the neuter name. This same *ekeinos* is emphasized in verse 14, where it is written out as the subject of the verb. Ordinarily the subject is inherent in the verb form itself. The added subject written out lends emphasis. "He and no one else shall glorify me." In verse 7, "I will send him unto you," the pronoun "him" (*auton*) is also masculine. It is quite clear, therefore, that Jesus himself regarded the Holy Spirit not as an "it" but as a "he," a person.

In the second place, the personality of the Holy Spirit is seen in his activities. He acts as a person. He dwells, teaches, guides, witnesses, speaks, hears, knows, wills, loves, glorifies, and gives (cf. John 14:17,26; 16:13–14; 1 Cor. 12:4 ff.). Likewise, the Holy Spirit reacts as a person. He can be grieved and blasphemed (Eph. 4:30; Matt. 12:31 f.). Furthermore, men react to the Holy Spirit as a person. He may be received, resisted, insulted, and glorified (John 20:22; Acts 7:51; 1 Peter 4:14).

The Scriptures, therefore, present the Holy Spirit as a personality. True, some see this personal element merely as an extension of the personalities of God and of Christ. There is an element of truth in this position. But it is only a portion of the truth. As will be seen presently the Holy Spirit also acts distinctively as a person of the Godhead.

God in Action

That the Holy Spirit is a divine person is seen in his relation to both God and Christ. This truth is evident in both the Old Testament and the New Testament.

Repeatedly in both Testaments the Spirit is called "the Spirit of God." Nowhere does the Spirit appear as an emanation or demigod coming out of God. At times he seems to be identified with God himself (Psalm 139:7; Isa. 63:10). And, yet, more often he is given an identity apart from God in the strictest sense (Gen. 1:2; Neh. 9:20; Psalm 51:11; Matt. 3:16). This does not mean that God and the Spirit are two distinct beings. Rather it means that the Spirit has functions which are distinct from God in the sense of Jehovah. The Spirit is God in action, sent forth to do God's bidding in the accomplishment of some specific end or purpose of God. As breath is a vital part of man yet is sent forth from man (e.g. in utterance), so is the Spirit identical with God but sent forth from God to do some specific work of God.

E. Y. Mullins summarizes the matter in this fashion: "The Spirit came upon individuals for specific purposes. The Spirit was thus God immanent in man and in the world. As the angel of the

Lord, or the angel of the Covenant in certain passages, represents both Jehovah Himself and one sent by Jehovah, so in like manner the Spirit of Jehovah was both Jehovah within or upon man, and at the same time one sent by Jehovah to man." [2]

The same interrelationship is seen between Christ and the Spirit. For instance, 1 Peter 1:11 speaks of the "Spirit of Christ" being in the Old Testament prophets when he "testified beforehand the sufferings of Christ, and the glory that should follow." Likewise, Paul speaks of the Holy Spirit as identical with Christ. In Romans 8:9, he compounds the picture as he refers to "the Spirit . . . the Spirit of God . . . the Spirit of Christ." This threefold relationship is also evident in 2 Corinthians 3:17: "Now the Lord is that Spirit: and where the Spirit of the Lord is, there is liberty." "Lord" refers to Jesus, and in this sense equates him with Jehovah. In all of these uses Paul is speaking in terms of deity. And in 1 Corinthians 15:45 he refers to Christ, the last Adam, as a "quickening" or "life-giving" Spirit. In each of these references there is an identification of Jesus Christ and the Holy Spirit.

Yet, the New Testament also refers to the Holy Spirit as a distinct person apart from Christ. In John 14:16, Jesus himself says, "I will pray the Father, and he shall give you another Comforter," referring to the Holy Spirit. Also the Spirit will teach concerning Jesus, he will glorify Jesus, and "he shall receive of mine [Jesus], and shall shew it unto you" (John 16:13–15; cf. John 15:26). This distinction Jesus further taught in Matthew 28:19. The disciples are to baptize "in the name of the Father, and of the Son, and of the Holy Ghost [Spirit]." And Paul repeats the same distinction of personality in 2 Corinthians 13:14: "The grace of the Lord Jesus Christ, and the love of God, and the communion of the Holy Ghost, be with you."

So the Bible teaches both an identification and a distinction in the Spirit's relation to both God and Jesus Christ. The identification does not destroy the personality of the Spirit any more than it destroys that of Jesus. Jesus is the Son of God. The Holy Spirit is the Spirit of both God and Christ. At the same time the distinction does not mean that there are three Gods. Each is a revelation of the one God doing the work of God. The distinction means that each personality of deity performs a specific function in accomplishing the purpose of God. The interrelation of the purpose involves the interrelation of the persons. Yet the specific differences of function imply the distinction. Nevertheless the interrelation also implies the deity of the Spirit along with that of both God and Christ.

The deity of the Holy Spirit is seen further in regard to his attributes. For as the Spirit of God he possesses the same attributes as those ascribed to God. Mullins divides these attributes into natural and moral.[3] The natural attributes are self-existence, immutability, omnipresence, omniscience, omnipotence, eternity, and immensity. The moral attributes are holiness, righteousness, love, and truth.

The Holy Spirit derives his being from no outside source. He exists by reason of who he is in himself. He is unchangeable in his nature and purpose. He is present in all of his power throughout space and time. The knowledge of the Spirit is complete, immediate, and simultaneous, with no necessity of thinking, reason, or inference. He is the expression of the power of God in operation. He is the eternal Spirit and is superior to space. He is neither confined to nor limited by space. Furthermore, the Holy Spirit is himself holiness, righteousness, truth, and love.

All in All—God

The word "trinity" does not appear in the Bible. But the doctrine is taught throughout the Bible. It is more clearly defined in the New Testament than in the Old. But the triune revelation is found in both Testaments. In the Old Testament God reveals himself as Jehovah, the angel of the Lord, and as the Spirit of Jehovah. In the New Testament he is seen as Father, Son, and Holy Spirit.

The Trinity does not mean that there are three Gods but one God, combining in himself three personalities or inner distinctions within the Godhead. It is difficult for man to comprehend this relationship. At the human level a person is a distinct individual separate from all other persons. However, even a man may in a sense be more than one personality. These distinctions may be more practical than inherent. For instance, the writer is husband, father, and pastor. And he bears all three relationships to his wife. He is her husband, the father of her child, and her pastor. Yet he is one man. But whereas man is finite, God is infinite. He is not less but more than man. In him, therefore, these distinctions in unity are infinite and perfect.

Theologians raise the question as to whether the Trinity is immanent or economic. Are these distinctions within the Godhead or are they merely outward manifestations to men? Mullins takes the position that they are immanent.[4] As thinking subject, infinite will, and eternal love, God requires an object. Such objects are the Son and the Spirit. But it also follows that these immanent distinctions find an economic expression as God reveals himself to men as Father, Son, and Spirit.

No earthly illustration can fully portray divine truth. But the following illustration is helpful in understanding the Trinity.

A survey of the Bible shows that in different parts of the Scriptures different persons of the Godhead occupy the more prominent position. Think of this revelation as a stage. In the Old Testament the Father is in the center of the stage, with the Son and Spirit on either side. In the Gospels, the Son is in the center of the stage, with the Father and Spirit on either side. Beginning with Acts, the Spirit is in the center of the stage, with the Father and Son on either side. Yet Father, Son, and Spirit are present at all times, and are involved in both the plot and the action.

To be sure, the Trinity is a mystery beyond man's full comprehension. If man could fully understand God, he could not worship him, for then he would be greater than God. Fully to understand anything, the mind must be greater than that which it understands. It must be able to envelop and subdue it. Finite mind can never do this to the infinite. But where the mind cannot go, faith can.

The Bible begins, "In the beginning God." It relates God's revelation as Father, Son, and Spirit. And at the point where the apostle Paul looks farther into the future than any other writer in the Bible, he sees a universe redeemed and subdued by God through Christ by the power of the Holy Spirit. "Then shall the Son also himself be subject unto him that put all things under him, that God may be all in all" (1 Cor. 15:28). God will still be Father, Son, and Holy Spirit. But we shall see him as he is— "God . . . all in all."

What He Does

2

As stated previously, the doctrine of the Holy Spirit is not defined as clearly in the Old Testament as it is in the New. For instance, the Trinity appears more definitely in the latter than in the former. Nevertheless, the Old Testament abundantly presents the Spirit and his place in the economy of God.

In Nature

The Holy Spirit is related to the natural order. This is first seen with regard to the creative act. The Bible assumes God in this act. Regardless of modern science's emphasis on secondary causes, behind it all stands God. "In the beginning God created the heaven and the earth." But the whole of creation was a chaos. However, in Genesis 1:2 we read that "the Spirit of God moved upon the face of the waters." The Hebrew word rendered "moved" means to brood or to hover, as a hen hovers over her young. In the King James Version of Deuteronomy 32:11 this same word is translated "fluttereth," an eagle fluttering over her young. The significance of the word in Genesis 1:2 is that the Holy Spirit hovered over the created chaos to give to it order and beauty, and to bring the cosmos toward the goal of a well-ordered universe.

Furthermore, the Spirit is related to the creation of things upon the earth. Psalm 104:30 reads, "Thou sendest forth thy spirit

[Spirit], they are created: and thou renewest the face of the earth." Likewise, the Spirit is said to have been active in setting in place the heavenly bodies. Job 26:13 says, "By his spirit he hath garnished the heavens."

A. B. Davidson translates this "by the Spirit of God the heavens are made bright." [1] He comments that this figure identifies the wind which carries away the clouds. But he relates this figure to "God's efficiency with the Spirit of God." However, the former meaning seems to be more natural. But in Isaiah 40:7 the hot winds are symbolic of the Spirit of the Lord. Also in Isaiah 32:15 the pouring out of the Spirit upon God's people shall make them as a fruitful field.

The dual meaning of *ruach* as wind and spirit served well the Old Testament writers to express the thought that the various natural phenomena were the result of the direct action of God's Spirit. This concept avoided both pantheism and polytheism. God was not a prisoner within nature, but outside and above it, and at the same time acting within or upon it. Furthermore, there were not many gods, but one God, acting in his several capacities in creation and in providence.

In the Life of Man

The Spirit of God is related to the life of man, both natural and spiritual. Here again the dual meaning of *ruach* lends itself to such a concept.

The Holy Spirit was involved in the making of man. Genesis 2:7 speaks of God's forming man out of the dust or chemical elements of the ground. Then he "breathed into his nostrils the breath of life; and man became a living soul [being]." Of course we should not think of God as a man doing a mouth-to-nose, life-giving act. The thought is that God is the source of life, and the Spirit gives it. As breath in man is an evidence of life, so God has life in himself. And he imparts it to man by his Spirit. David-

son notes that "man's life is the presence in man of God's
Spirit." [2] Thus in Job 33:4, Elihu says, "The spirit of God hath
made me, and the breath of the Almighty hath given me life." In
a parallelism, Job 27:3 combines the two ideas, both natural and
spiritual. "All the while my breath is in me, and the spirit of God
is in my nostrils."

The psalmist has a similar picture of God's Spirit as the source
of life, but of that spirit or breath in man as man's spirit. Psalm
104:29–30 reads, "Thou hidest thy face, they are troubled: thou
takest away their breath, they die, and return to their dust. Thou
sendest forth thy spirit, they are created" (cf. Ezek. 37:14;
39:29). And again in Job 34:14–15, Elihu summarizes the whole.
"If he set his heart upon man [if God should set His mind on
Himself; i.e., cease to think of the creature],[3] if he gather unto
himself his spirit and his breath; all flesh shall perish together,
and man shall turn again unto dust."

The Old Testament also sees the Spirit of God as the source of
man's spiritual life or his likeness to God himself. "God said, Let
us make man in our image, after our likeness. . . . So God
created man in his own image" (Gen. 1:26–27).

Two things should be noted. The "us" and "our" in verse 26
should not necessarily be used as an argument for the Trinity,
even though the concept is true. These are more likely plural
pronouns of majesty. However, combining these verses with
Genesis 2:7, it is also clear that the Holy Spirit is involved in the
act. For it was through the imparting of his Spirit to man that
man himself became a living spirit. It is in this sense that man is
made in God's image and after his likeness. Through the Holy
Spirit, man is more than an animal possessing the animal principle
of life. He is also a finite spiritual being, a personality, even as
God is infinite spirit and personality. The source of this enduement of man is the Spirit of God.

Of further interest is Genesis 6:3: "My spirit shall not always strive with man." "Strive" also means "rule." The sense of this verse is that the Spirit acts within the moral nature of man. Thus the Holy Spirit not only gives to man his moral and spiritual being but continues to act within it. Even so, man is a personality with the right of choice. The Spirit will not violate man's personality. He can choose, but is responsible for his choices.

In Deeds of Service

One of the chief functions of the Holy Spirit in the Old Testament has to do with services for God performed by various individuals. Mullins reminds us that these services involved the covenant relation between Jehovah and Israel.[4] Any extraordinary powers, regardless of their nature, which were exhibited by the Israelites were attributed to the Holy Spirit.

One such service was the conferring of power upon judges and warriors for a specific function. For instance, Judges 3:10 says, "The Spirit of the Lord came upon him [Othniel], and he judged Israel, and went out to war . . . and his hand prevailed." The Spirit came upon Gideon, and he defeated the Midianites, and upon Jephthah to do mighty works (Judg. 6:34; 11:29).

Of Gideon it is of interest to note that the Spirit *clothed himself with him* (cf. 1 Chron. 12:18; 2 Chron. 24:20). He put on Gideon as a garment, suggesting the close relationship between the Spirit and Gideon.

Samson is mentioned repeatedly as being used of the Spirit. "The Spirit of the Lord *began to move* [stir] him at times in the camp of Dan" (Judg. 13:25, author's italics). Davies notes that this verb connotes a striking, hitting, impelling activity.[5] It is as though the Spirit poked him in the ribs to arouse him to the needs of his people. A picturesque word is used of Samson in Judges 14:6: "The Spirit of the Lord came mightily upon him" (cf. Judg. 14:19; 15:14). The Hebrew verb connotes a sweeping, leaping movement as the Spirit rushed or pounced upon him, enabling him to do mighty deeds.

The Spirit was involved in God's choice of Saul to be the king over Israel. When Samuel anointed him he said that "the Spirit of the Lord will come upon thee, and thou shalt prophesy with them, and shalt be turned into another man" (1 Sam. 10:6). But when Saul proved to be unfaithful, at God's command Samuel anointed David to be king. The Spirit of the Lord then came upon him, but departed from Saul (16:13–14).

In all of these instances it is evident that the Spirit was given with no necessary reference to the moral character of the recipient. The enduement was with reference to the covenant relationship between Jehovah and Israel. In time of the nation's need Jehovah was faithful to his covenant to deliver and guide through men of his choosing in a given situation. But the primary relationship in each case was not between Jehovah and a man. It was that between him and his people.

Another service of the Spirit was to endow certain men with skills necessary to perform a stated service. Having received Joseph's prediction of the seven years of want, Pharaoh proceeded to make preparations for it. According to Joseph's suggestion, he must choose someone to direct the enterprise. But, he asked, "Can we find such a one as this is, a man in whom the Spirit of God is? . . . Forasmuch as God hath shewed thee all this, there is none so discreet and wise as thou art" (Gen. 41:38–39). Thus the insight and administrative ability of Joseph was recognized as a gift of the Spirit.

Again, when God told Moses to make the tabernacle, its contents, and the various accouterments for worship, he said to the leader of Israel, "I have called by name Bezaleel . . . and I have filled him with the spirit of God, in wisdom, and in understanding, and in knowledge, and in all manner of workmanship, to devise cunning works, to work in gold, and in silver, and in brass, and in cutting of stones, to set them, and in carving of timber, to work in all manner of workmanship" (Ex. 31:2–5; cf. Ex. 28:3; 35:31; 1 Kings 7:14; 2 Chron. 2:14). Therefore, the Holy Spirit is the source of the various skills needed for this sacred task. This thought places an aura of glory about all such endeavors.

The Spirit also seems to have been related to the ability of leadership. God instructed Moses to select as his successor "Joshua the son of Nun, a man in whom is the spirit" (Num. 27:18). This ability is further seen in Deuteronomy 34:9: "Joshua the son of Nun was full of the spirit of wisdom; for Moses had laid his hands upon him: and the children of Israel hearkened unto him, and did as the Lord commanded Moses." Note this Old Testament parallel to the New Testament practice of receiving the Spirit by the laying on of hands (cf. Acts 8:17).

Daniel's ability to interpret Nebuchadnezzar's dream and the handwriting on the wall of Belshazzar's banquet hall is attributed to the Spirit. And this ability finally led to his being placed in a position of power (Dan. 4:8; 5:11 ff.; 6:13). Furthermore, the presence of the Spirit enabled Zerubbabel to build the postexilic Temple in Jerusalem (Zech. 4:6 ff.).

A review of the work of the Spirit in enabling men to do specific tasks shows a progression from the lower to the higher. The former involved power to do mighty works. The latter work was largely to heighten the natural skills of a man to a degree beyond man himself through spiritually endowed abilities. There remains yet a third function of the Spirit in empowering men to serve Jehovah's purpose. This function was in the realm of prophecy.

The basic element in prophecy was that of speaking forth for God, the delivering of his message. Thus both Abraham and Moses are called prophets (Gen. 20:7; Deut. 18:15). But the role of the prophet early came to be recognized as that of one who possessed the Spirit of God. For instance, even though Hosea's enemies taunted him, "the prophet is a fool," they still recognized him as a "spiritual man" or "a man of the spirit" (Hos. 9:7).

The earliest form of prophecy as such was accompanied by an excited ecstasy, often associated with or brought on by the use of musical instruments. Such an example is found in 1 Samuel 10:5. In the following verse Samuel promises that Saul will prophesy, a promise that in verses 10-11 was recorded as fulfilled shortly. This was ascribed to "the Spirit of the Lord" coming upon him. However, in 1 Samuel 18:10 it is said that "the evil spirit from God came upon Saul, and he prophesied in the . . . house."

Two questions arise at this point. First, was the aforementioned prophecy akin to that of the later prophets? The contents of the prophesying is not given, therefore it is impossible to judge fully. Perhaps the only definite thing shown by this is that such ecstatic utterance was at that time associated with the Spirit of God. Second, what may we understand by the Lord's sending an evil spirit resulting in prophecy? There are other instances when an evil or lying spirit is mentioned as coming from Jehovah (cf. 1 Sam. 16:14; 19:9; 1 Kings 22:19 ff.).

Two things may be noted about this. A certain type of utterance was called prophecy, whether its message was true or false. The ancients thought of everything coming from Jehovah. Hence this concept of an evil or lying spirit. Again, the more probable answer is that Jehovah's *sending* such a spirit may be seen as God's permissive will rather than his intended will. When a man rebels against God's Spirit and follows his own rebellious spirit to do evil, God *permits* it but does not *cause* it.

The highest form of the Spirit's activity with respect to prophecy is seen in what we call the major and minor prophets. The usual form used in presenting their messages was "Thus saith the Lord or Jehovah" or some equivalent phrase (cf. Isa.

49:5; Jer. 1:8; Amos 2:11). Thus Jehovah by his Spirit spoke through the prophets. In this sense Isaiah 1:2 begins his prophecy, "Hear, O heavens, and give ear, O earth: for the Lord hath spoken." Jeremiah 1:4 notes that "the word of the Lord came unto" him to tell him that even while Jeremiah was still in his mother's womb, Jehovah had called him to be a prophet. Ezekiel 1:3 says that "the word of the Lord came expressly upon" him in Chaldea.

The action of the Spirit is clearly and repeatedly mentioned in Ezekiel. Ezekiel 2:2 says that "the spirit entered into" him to commission him to prophesy to "the children of Israel." In 8:2–3, the Spirit is described as the "hand" of Jehovah taking the prophet by the hair and transporting him to Jerusalem. There the Spirit fell upon Ezekiel so that he prophesied to the nation (chap. 11). His vision of the valley of dry bones came through the Spirit (chap. 37). Throughout this prophecy the Spirit takes the prophet here and there to prophesy by both word and demonstration.

The entire picture of the place of the Spirit in prophecy may be summed up in the words of Micah 3:8. "But truly I am full of power by the spirit of the Lord, and of judgment, and of might, to declare unto Jacob his transgression, and to Israel his sin." One has but to refer to Isaiah 40 and 53 to see the Spirit's role in bringing comfort and salvation to a repentant people.

In Moral and Spiritual Character

This role of the Spirit is implied in words used to qualify his name. He is the "holy" Spirit not only as to what he is but in that which he imparts (cf. Psalm 51:11; Isa. 63:10). In the wilderness God gave his "good spirit to instruct" Israel (Neh. 9:20). The psalmist prayed, "Teach me to do thy will; for thou art my God; thy spirit is good; lead me into the land of uprightness" (Psalm 143:10).

The ethical function of the Holy Spirit is abundantly taught in the prophets. Isaiah 44:3–5 likens the Spirit to water for a thirsty man and land, bringing renewal:

For I will pour water upon him that is thirsty, and floods upon the dry ground: I will pour my spirit upon thy seed, and my blessing upon thine offspring: And they shall spring up as among the grass, as willows by the water courses. One shall say, I am the Lord's; and another shall call himself by the name of Jacob; and another shall subscribe with his hand unto the Lord, and surname himself by the name of Israel.

Spiritual cleansing is taught by a similar figure in Ezekiel: "Then will I sprinkle clean water upon you, and ye shall be clean: . . . A new heart also will I give you, and a new spirit will I put within you: . . . And I will put my spirit within you, and cause you to walk in my statutes, and ye shall keep my judgments, and do them" (36:25–27). "The spirit of grace and of supplications" is promised in Zechariah 12:10.

There is no more poignant prayer in the Old Testament than that found in Psalm 51:11. In an overwhelming sense of guilt, David prays, "Cast me not away from thy presence; and take not thy holy spirit from me." He is so vile that he fears that God's presence, the Holy Spirit, can no longer abide in him. This should not be interpreted in the light of the New Testament sense of the Holy Spirit indwelling the believer. But it clearly shows the Old Testament teaching of the intricate relationship between the Holy Spirit and moral and spiritual character.

In Relation to the Messiah

The Old Testament presents the Messiah as being anointed and empowered for his work. This is seen especially in Isaiah. Of course, there are those who insist that these "Suffering Servant" pictures relate only to the remnant of Judah coming out of the Babylonian captivity. But when read in the light of the Christian revelation, they clearly point beyond the remnant to the higher picture of the Messiah himself. For instance, if these passages be limited only to the remnant, there is no event in all of history which fulfils Isaiah 53.

Thus the Holy Spirit is seen as anointing the Messiah for his work. Isaiah 42:1 says, "Behold my servant, whom I uphold; mine elect, in whom my soul delighteth; I have put my spirit upon him: he shall bring forth judgment to the Gentiles." Verses 2–7 tell how the Spirit-anointed Messiah will do his work.

In Isaiah 61:1–3, this picture is even more vividly portrayed. In Luke 4, Jesus quoted a portion of this passage with reference to himself: "The Spirit of the Lord God is upon me; because the Lord hath anointed me to preach good tidings unto the meek; he hath sent me to bind up the brokenhearted, to proclaim liberty to the captives, and the opening of the prison to them that are bound; to proclaim the acceptable year of the Lord, . . . to give unto them beauty for ashes, . . . that they might be called trees of righteousness, the planting of the Lord, that he might be glorified."

Furthermore, the Messiah is seen as endowed with gifts by the Holy Spirit. Isaiah 11:1–5 delineates this truth:

There shall come forth a rod out of the stem of Jesse, and a Branch shall grow out of his roots: And the spirit of the Lord shall rest upon him, the spirit of wisdom and understanding, the spirit of counsel and might, the spirit of knowledge and of the fear of the Lord; and shall make him of quick understanding in the fear of the Lord: and he shall not judge after the sight of his eyes, neither reprove after the hearing of his ears: But with righteousness shall he judge the poor, and reprove with equity for the meek of the earth: and he shall smite the earth with the rod of his mouth, and with the breath of his lips shall he slay the wicked. And righteousness shall be the girdle of his loins, and faithfulness the girdle of his reins.

These passages clearly show that not a people but a person is

involved. They point to the work of the Messiah as being related to the power of the Spirit. And they find complete fulfilment in the ministry of Jesus Christ.

In Historical Perspective

The Old Testament promises a future ministry of the Spirit, a
ministry which finds its full expression in the New Testament.
Thus the Old Testament gives but a foretaste of a higher work of
the Holy Spirit. The promise of this work is threefold.

First, it relates to the seed of Jacob. Isaiah 44:3–4 says, "I
will pour my spirit upon thy seed, and my blessing upon thine
offspring: And they shall spring up as among the grass, as willows
by the water courses."

The immediate historical context is a promise to Judah regarding the postexilic period. Taken by itself it might be confined
to the remnant. But in the larger context it becomes a promise
regarding the true seed of Jacob, as seen in the Christian family.
So the time is coming when through the Spirit this seed will truly
flourish "as willows by the water courses" or as the sands of the
sea. And this will be made possible through him who is anointed
of God as the Redeemer (cf. 1 Peter 2:3–10).

Second, the promise is related to the Redeemer. "The Redeemer shall come to Zion, and unto them that turn from transgression in Jacob, saith the Lord. As for me, this is my covenant
with them, saith the Lord; My spirit that is upon thee [Re-
deemer], and my words which I have put in thy mouth, shall not
depart out of thy mouth, nor out of the mouth of thy seed, nor
out of the mouth of thy seed's seed, saith the Lord, from henceforth and for ever" (Isa. 59:20–21).

The work of the Redeemer shall be by the power of the Holy
Spirit. And through his seed the Spirit shall continue the work of
redemption as it is proclaimed to a lost world. What the Redeemer
began in the Spirit's power, the Spirit will continue, as in mighty

power he comes upon "them that turn from transgression in Jacob."

Third, the promise is related to the redeemed. Joel 2:28 says, "I will pour out my spirit upon all flesh." This is the Old Testament promise of the New Testament Pentecost. This entire passage in Joel 2:28–32 is cited by Peter as being fulfilled on the day of Pentecost (Acts 2:16 ff.).

Following that experience, Spirit-possessed men went forth to challenge a lost world to turn to God who was in Christ reconciling the world unto himself. Thus he who was divine power, sent forth from God in the beginning to bring order out of chaos in the natural creation, took the center of the stage in his mighty act of spiritual re-creation. This he will continue to do until the end of time. It is this truth which combines into one whole the teaching concerning the Holy Spirit in both the New Testament and in the Old Testament.

The Account in the Gospels

3

The New Testament is the flower and fruit of God's revelation, whose roots are firmly planted in the fertile soil of the Old Testament. It is natural, therefore, that the revelation is clearer in the new than in the old covenant.

God reveals himself progressively, as man is capable of receiving and understanding the revelation. Thus we expect to see a clearer picture of God and his redemptive purpose in John than in Genesis. The *promised* redemption of the Old Testament is the *provided* redemption in the New Testament. The *prophesied* Messiah of the Old Testament becomes the *personified* Christ of the New Testament.

It is to be expected, therefore, that the Spirit of God in the Old Testament comes into clearer focus in the New Testament. Even this picture becomes more pronounced as we proceed through the Gospels, the Acts, the Epistles, and the Revelation.

As in the Old Testament, here also the Holy Spirit is God's Spirit sent forth to perform his specific work. Detailed facets of the Spirit's work will be treated in subsequent chapters.

In the Gospels the Holy Spirit is seen as working upon, in, and through Jesus Christ. Through the teachings of Jesus they also anticipate the further work which the Spirit will do in and through the disciples.

The Holy Spirit is the generating power of God in the virgin birth of Jesus. As he is the giver of life to man, even so, he is the conceiver of the life of the Son of God in his historical appearance as Jesus Christ. In simple language, and without fanfare, Matthew 1:18 says that before Mary "came together" with Joseph, "she was found with child of the Holy Ghost [Spirit]." Finding her in this condition, out of wedlock, Joseph was greatly troubled. He accepted the situation only after the Lord appeared to him in a dream, saying, "That which is conceived in her is of the Holy Spirit" (v.20).

Luke is even more specific in his account. The angel Gabriel appeared to the virgin Mary to announce the forthcoming birth of "the Son of the Highest." In response to Mary's inquiry as to how this could be, since she knew not a man (The verb "know," present tense of continued action, in Luke 1:34 clearly denotes her present virginity and her resolve to remain thus so long as she was out of wedlock.), the angel said, "The Holy Ghost [Spirit] shall come upon thee, and the power of the Highest shall overshadow thee: therefore also that holy thing which shall be born of thee shall be called the Son of God" (v.35; note "Son of the Highest," v.32, and "power of the Highest," v.35).

Luke's record is all the more significant since he was a physician. In the introduction to his Gospel he states that before writing he "traced the course of all things accurately from the first" (1:3, ASV). It is even possible that he received the birth narrative from Mary herself. This physician fully records the virgin birth of Jesus and attributes it to the Holy Spirit.

The conception of Jesus by the Holy Spirit speaks of his sinless nature. A certain school of theology would attribute this nature to the sinlessness of Mary. But there is no biblical basis for such a claim. Mullins is right when he says, "The sinlessness of Jesus was not due to the sinlessness of His mother, but to the Divine origin of His human nature, the Spirit of God." [1]

Notice should also be taken of a further work of the Holy

Spirit in connection with the birth and infancy of Jesus. He revealed the fact of the virgin conception to Mary's cousin Elizabeth. Shortly after the angel's visit to her, Mary visited her cousin, who also was with child through supernatural means (Luke 1:5–25; cf. Luke 1:67 ff.). Upon being greeted by Mary, Elizabeth's child leaped in her womb. Whereupon she "was filled with the Holy Ghost [Spirit]" (v.41) and blessed Mary and the fruit of her womb, calling Mary "the mother of my Lord" (v.43).

In the Temple in Jerusalem was the aged saint Simeon, upon whom was the Holy Spirit who had revealed to him that he should live until he had seen the Lord's Christ. He was led by the Spirit to the Temple at the time the infant Jesus was presented. Seeing Jesus, he acclaimed him as the one bringing salvation to Israel and to the Gentiles, even predicting by inference the manner in which salvation would be provided (2:25–35).

While the Spirit is not mentioned by name, it is apparent that he was active in the dreams of the magi, and also in those of Joseph, which led to the sojourn in Egypt and return to Nazareth (Matt. 2:12–23). During the silent years in Nazareth the Spirit was active in the development of the child Jesus (Luke 2:40,52).

Furthermore, the Holy Spirit appears in a peculiar way at the baptism of Jesus. As Jesus approached his thirtieth birthday, John the Baptist in the wilderness of Judea was heralding the Coming One as one who would baptize "with the Holy Ghost [Spirit], and with fire" (Matt. 3:11). Frank Stagg notes the distinction drawn between John and Jesus. John could herald the coming King and kingdom, calling for repentance and faith. But "only 'the Coming One,' i.e., Jesus Christ, could bring the Holy Spirit" for his peculiar work in the redemptive purpose of God.[2]

Finally, Jesus himself appeared on the scene to be baptized by John. Even though there is no record that the Baptist had known Jesus heretofore, his Spirit-enlightened mind sensed his identity. He had been told of God that the one on whom he saw the Spirit descending would be the Christ (John 1:32–34). When John baptized Jesus "the heavens were opened unto him, and he [and John] saw the Spirit of God descending like a dove, and lighting upon him" (Matt. 3:16–17; cf. Mark 1:10). Luke says that "the Holy Ghost [Spirit] descended in a bodily shape like a dove upon him" (Luke 3:22).

The presence of the Trinity was inferred in Gabriel's message to Mary, but here the distinct persons of the Trinity are mentioned—Jesus (Son), God or Father (voice), and Holy Spirit (dove). Though distinct, these manifestations of God were intimately identified in the redemptive work set forth in the Gospels.

How may we understand the coming of the Holy Spirit upon Jesus at this time? In Hebrew thought the dove is symbolic of gentleness, innocence, and meekness. The Spirit is the essence of divine power. Also the Levitical law prescribed one dove, along with a lamb, or two doves only for the poor, as a sacrificial offering. Therefore, the anointing of Jesus by the Spirit probably suggests three things. First, Jesus is the essence of gentleness, innocence, and meekness. Second, he is to work in the power of the Spirit. Third, he is to be the sacrifice for sin. Jesus, the Lamb, and the Holy Spirit, the Dove, are both involved in this sacrifice and Jesus' resurrection from the dead (cf. Rom. 1:4; Heb. 9:14). The approving voice of the Father is involved in all of this redemptive act. Jesus' baptism symbolized the entire thing. And at the outset of his ministry the Father, Son, and Holy Spirit are manifested as being present in it.

Why should the Holy Spirit come upon the Son in a special way at his baptism? Obviously it was to anoint Jesus, the King, the Anointed One or Messiah, for his work. Until now the Holy Spirit had worked upon Jesus. Jesus was God; he was also man. His human nature needed this enduement of the power of God sent forth through God's Spirit.

E. Y. Mullins notes that the bodily shape as a dove suggests the totality of God's Spirit.[3] To the disciples at Pentecost the Spirit was given distributively and partially, as suggested by the cloven tongues as of fire. But John 3:34 says, "For he whom God hath sent speaketh the words of God: for God giveth not the Spirit by measure unto him." He gave him in his fulness. And the fact that the Holy Spirit came upon Jesus in fulness also means that Jesus is qualified to bestow the Spirit upon his disciples (cf. Matt. 3:11; John 20:22; Acts 1:5).

The Holy Spirit is involved in the temptation experience of Jesus in the wilderness. Having been anointed for his ministry, it was now necessary to determine what kind of Messiah he would be. This is the focal point in each of the temptations.[4] So Matthew 4:1 says, "Then was Jesus led up of the Spirit into the wilderness to be tempted of the devil." Mark 1:12 uses the stronger term, "The Spirit driveth him into the wilderness." Matthew's "to be tempted" or "tried" is an infinitive of purpose. So the initiative in the trial was God's, not that of the devil.

Luke 4:1 notes that Jesus, being full of the Holy Spirit, returned from the Jordan. Then, literally, he says "And was led in the Spirit in the wilderness forty days being tempted." This suggests that the Spirit not only led or drove Jesus into the wilderness but continued to lead him throughout the entire experience. Jesus resisted the devil in his human nature, but it was by the power of the Holy Spirit. He resisted the devil by the use of the Scriptures, the sword of the Spirit. And when he triumphed over the tempter, "angels came and ministered unto him" (Matt. 4:11). This also suggests a ministry of the Holy Spirit. This was not to be the last temptation nor the last ministry of the Holy Spirit. In fact, even when not specifically stated, the Gospels, and especially Luke, imply that all of Jesus' ministry was in the power of the Holy Spirit.

Certain passages may be cited in which specific mention is

made concerning the Holy Spirit in Jesus' public ministry. For
instance, Luke 4:14 introduces Jesus' Galilean ministry by saying,
"Jesus returned in the power of the Spirit into Galilee." There
follows a brief summary of his ministry. Then he records Jesus'
visit to Nazareth. In the synagogue Jesus read Isaiah 61:1–2,
which begins with the significant words, "The Spirit of the Lord
is upon me, because he hath anointed me" (Luke 4:18–19).
There followed a list of the works to be performed by the Messiah.
Then Jesus commented, "This day is this scripture fulfilled in your
ears" (Luke 4:21). The people were astonished to hear such a
claim from one of their neighbors. But subsequent events were
to prove its truth.

Jesus was to see the Spirit working even in his followers. Upon
the return of the seventy who reported that even demons or evil
spirits were subject unto them through Jesus' name, he "rejoiced
in spirit [the Holy Spirit, best manuscripts], and said, I thank
thee, O Father, Lord of heaven and earth, that thou hast hid
these things from the wise and prudent, and hast revealed them
unto babes" (Luke 10:21).

He "returned in the power of the [Holy] Spirit into Galilee:
. . . and he taught in their synagogues" (Luke 4:14–15). Jesus
taught by the Holy Spirit. Furthermore, he said, "The words that
I speak unto you, they are spirit, and they are life" (John 6:63).

The miracles of Jesus were wrought in the power of the Holy
Spirit. The apocryphal or noncanonical gospels picture the child
Jesus performing all kinds of miracles, stories which are silly and
without meaning or purpose. But the canonical Gospels do not
show any miracle until after Jesus' anointing by the Spirit at his
baptism. Thereafter he wrought many miracles whose very purpose and simplicity attest their genuineness.

In Matthew 12:18–21, after healing a withered hand, Jesus
cited Isaiah 42:1–3, which contains the phrase "I will put my
spirit upon him." This entire passage beautifully describes the

tenderness and patience with which Jesus ministered to human needs. And it clearly relates the Holy Spirit to this ministry.

In the passage which follows this, Matthew records how Jesus cast demons out of a man (vv.22–37). The Pharisees attributed this obviously good work to "Beelzebub the prince of demons." Whereupon Jesus proceeded to teach the terrible lesson about blaspheming the Holy Spirit, which within itself shows how intimately the Holy Spirit was identified with the miraculous works of Jesus.

Blasphemy against the Holy Spirit is called the unpardonable sin. Matthew 12:31–32 contains the darkest words which ever fell from Jesus' lips. The fact that they came from him who is infinite love and mercy makes them all the more terrible. Therefore, we shall do well to consider them at length.

"All manner of sin and blasphemy shall be forgiven unto men: but the blasphemy against the Holy Ghost [Spirit ("Holy" not in best manuscripts, but genuine in verse 32)] shall not be forgiven unto men. . . . whosoever speaketh a word against the Son of man, it shall be forgiven him: but whosoever speaketh against the Holy Ghost [Spirit], it shall not be forgiven him, neither in this world [age], neither in the world [age] to come."

Blasphemy comes from the Greek word *blasphēmeō,* which means to speak slanderously or insultingly so as to defame one's character or reputation. Note that all such speaking may be forgiven, except that against the Holy Spirit. But for blasphemy against the Holy Spirit there is no promise of forgiveness in this present age nor in the age to come.

Now what constitutes this sin? There are many popular but false assumptions regarding it. It is not blasphemy against either the Father or the Son. It is not murder nor any other sin committed in a fit of anger. While rejecting Christ until death is unpardonable, this is not the sin involved here. It is a sin committed in life. Occasionally a Christian may feel that he has committed this sin. But such is impossible, since the Christian is already saved in Christ and is sealed unto full redemption by the Holy Spirit (cf. Eph. 1:13–14). The fact that a person is conscious of sin is evidence that he has not committed this sin. That sense of sin is evidence that the Holy Spirit is still dealing with him through conviction (cf. John 16:8 ff.). None of these sins fits the context of Jesus' words about the unpardonable sin.

Jesus said that "a word against the Son of man . . . shall be forgiven" (Matt. 12:32). It is blasphemy against the Holy Spirit which is unpardonable. Note that Jesus used the word "Holy" as though to contrast the Spirit with the *evil* spirit of Satan.

An examination of the event will help us to understand the nature of the unpardonable sin. Jesus had performed an unmistakably good work by the power of the Holy Spirit. The people recognized it as such. But the Pharisees attributed it to Satan. This implied that to them it was an evil work. So to them good was evil and evil was good. Like Satan, in *Paradise Lost,* they said, "Evil, be thou my good." They had so hardened themselves that they had lost the power of moral discrimination.

Several things may be said about their sin. First, it was not a sin of impulse. It came as the result of a long process of resisting Jesus and his work. Second, it was a sin of knowledge. The people saw the miracle and attributed it to God's power. The Pharisees saw it and attributed it to Satan. Third, it was a sin of deliberate choice.

Seeing the miracle, the Pharisees had to decide whether Jesus worked by God's Holy Spirit or by Satan's evil spirit. They chose to attribute it to Satan's spirit. In so doing they rejected the Holy Spirit. And since he is both the Spirit of God and the Spirit of Christ, in rejecting him they rejected Deity himself. They did not merely *resist* the Spirit, as did Saul of Tarsus, and later surrender to him. In their opposition to Jesus they fully and finally *rejected* God's Holy Spirit. And since he is the convicting power of the

Godhead, they had no consciousness of sin! No conviction, no repentance! No repentance, no faith. No faith, no salvation! The unpardonable sin!

Is it possible to commit this sin today? It is the conviction of the author that it is. A man through repeated refusal of the wooing of the Holy Spirit can become so crusted in his spirit that he loses all sense of moral discrimination. To him, good becomes evil and evil becomes good. Thus he loses all sense of sin. He rejects the Holy Spirit, he turns from Deity himself. Thus he sins the sin of deliberate choice, and in the light of full knowledge, whereby he fully and finally rejects God and chooses the will and way of Satan.

The climax of the Gospels is the death and resurrection of Jesus. There is no specific mention in the Gospels that the Holy Spirit was involved in these events. But Hebrews 9:14 says that Christ "through the eternal Spirit offered himself without spot to God." And Romans 1:4 says that Jesus Christ was "declared to be the Son of God with power, according to the spirit of holiness, by the resurrection from the dead" (cf. Rom. 8:11). These two references are sufficient to establish the fact of the Spirit's work in these redemptive acts of God in Christ Jesus.

It is of special significance to note the place of the Holy Spirit in the various commissions of Jesus to his disciples. The first of these is recorded in John 20:21–22. On resurrection Sunday night Jesus appeared to ten of the apostles. After giving physical evidence of his bodily resurrection, he said, "As my Father hath sent me, even so send I you. And when he had said this, he breathed on them [cf. Gen. 2:7], and saith unto them, Receive ye the Holy Ghost [Spirit]." John the Baptist had said that he would baptize with the Holy Spirit (Matt. 3:11). So completely was Jesus filled with the Holy Spirit that now he imparts him to his apostles. And with this gift went power to do their work (John 20:23). Thus, in a sense, Jesus gave them a foretaste of Pentecost.

The second commission was given to the apostles and others on a mountain in Galilee. "All power [authority] is given unto me in heaven and in earth. Go ye therefore, and teach [disciple] all nations, baptizing them in the name of the Father, and of the Son, and of the Holy Ghost [Spirit] . . . teaching them . . . and, lo, I am with you always, even unto the end of the world [age]" (Matt. 28:18–20).

Four things are worthy of note. First, authority renders a word meaning "out of being" (*exousia*). Out of his very being as the resurrected Lord, Jesus gave this commission. And his resurrection was by "the spirit of holiness." Second, the basic commission is to "disciple all nations." This work will be done by the power of the Holy Spirit. Third, the disciples are to baptize in the name of the Father, Son, and Holy Spirit, the triune God. They are to teach, which itself will be done through the Spirit (John 14:26). Fourth, Jesus promised his abiding presence, a presence which is through the Holy Spirit (John 14:16–18).

The final commission found in the Gospels is recorded in Luke 24:47–49 (cf. Acts 1:5,8). Beginning in Jerusalem the apostles are to bear witness to Jesus' redeeming work. For this work he promises the Holy Spirit. "Tarry ye in the city of Jerusalem, until ye be endued with power from on high." Literally, "until ye get yourselves clothed with power from on high."

The Holy Spirit will come upon them in accord with the Father's promise. But they must *get themselves clothed* with his power. This suggests a moral and spiritual preparation on their part in order that they may be used of the Spirit. We may well imagine that the days intervening before Pentecost were spent in confessing their sins, mending broken fellowship, and dedicating themselves to God's will and purpose. When the Holy Spirit came, they were ready, willing, and available.

With regard to the Holy Spirit in the Gospels one final matter remains—Jesus' promises as to the Holy Spirit and the disciples themselves. In Luke 11:13, he assures them that the Heavenly Father will give the Holy Spirit to them that ask him. In Luke 12:11–12, he gives a definite promise as to the Spirit's presence and help in time of need but says nothing about their asking for it: "When they bring you unto the synagogues, and unto magistrates, and powers, take ye no thought how or what thing ye shall answer, or what ye shall say: For the Holy Ghost [Spirit] shall teach you in the same hour what ye ought to say" (cf. Matt. 10:20; Mark 13:11). Matthew 10:20 plainly says that "it is not ye that speak, but the Spirit of your Father which speaketh in you." The Spirit speaks through the disciples.

This should not be used to justify a lack of preparation before preaching, teaching, or otherwise speaking for the Lord. The promise relates to a time of persecution. The Holy Spirit acts as the advocate or paraclete (cf. John 14:16) of the disciple who is brought before some religious or political tribunal.

W. Hersey Davis comments on this promise: "When they are called to defend themselves before hostile authorities, they are promised the special aid of the Holy Spirit. They are not to be anxiously considering the plan and delivery of their defense and its subject matter, for all this will be given to them by the Holy Spirit. This special promise is given because they have not had time or opportunity to thoroughly survey the grounds of faith; they are not ready to argue and plead." [5]

The burden of Jesus' words in John 14–16 deals with the promise and work of the Holy Spirit in and for the disciples after his ascension into heaven. These matters will be treated in detail in later chapters of this volume.

Looking back on the work of the Holy Spirit in the Gospels, it is clear that Jesus was thoroughly endued with his power. In a sense the picture continues that of the Old Testament wherein the Spirit of God acted upon and in chosen vessels. There are two differences, however. Whereas in the Old Testament the Spirit came in measure upon men for some specific purpose, he dwelt in Jesus without measure and was active in all of his works.

Furthermore, whereas in the Old Testament fillings of the Spirit the Spirit himself was the more prominent figure; in the Gospels Jesus is made the more prominent. Mullins sums it up for us in the following words. "In the Gospels the view is concentrated less upon the Spirit than upon Jesus Himself, though it is always assumed that He is acting in the power of the Spirit. In the case of Jesus also, the moral quality of His words and deeds is always assumed." [6]

Acts to Revelation

4

When we pass from the Gospels into the remainder of the New Testament literature, we are conscious of a change in atmosphere. It is an atmosphere supercharged with the Holy Spirit. This does not deny his previous activity. Neither does it mean that we leave the Father and Son behind. All three persons of the Trinity are present. But to recall our figure, the Holy Spirit is in the center of the stage with the Father and Son on either side. It is impossible to isolate one from the other.

As in the Old Testament, so in the New. At times the Spirit is identical with the Father and Son; at other times the Spirit is seen acting in his individual capacity.

In the Gospels (especially in John), the major emphasis is upon the Son, moving in the power of the Father and/or the Spirit. Beyond that point the major emphasis is upon the Holy Spirit, working through the disciples in the spread of the gospel and in the hammering out of Christian doctrine. Of course, in all of this the Father and Son are prominent. But still the power is that of the Holy Spirit. This is as Jesus said it would be (cf. John 14–16).

We shall reserve many details of the Holy Spirit's work for a closer look in subsequent chapters. But for the present, let us continue our survey of the Holy Spirit as he appears in the remainder of the New Testament.

The Acts of the Apostles

The book of Acts has been called "the Gospel of the Holy Spirit." This is based largely upon two things. First, it is derived from the opening verses of Acts. Luke's Gospel obviously is the gospel of Jesus Christ, even though the Holy Spirit figures prominently in it. In fact, more than any other Gospel, Luke places emphasis upon the Holy Spirit working through Jesus.

Luke begins Acts by referring to "the former treatise" in which he had recorded "all that Jesus began both to do and teach" (1:1). Then he points beyond the ascension to the work which continued through the followers of Jesus. The Lord had promised the special coming of the Holy Spirit (John 14:16–17). Before his ascension he told the apostles to wait for this promise to be fulfilled (Acts 1:4). They were to "be baptized with the Holy Ghost [Spirit] not many days hence" (v.5). And through the power which they received from him they were to evangelize the world (v.8). So that which Jesus began among his disciples the Holy Spirit was to continue through them.

Second, the term "the Gospel of the Holy Spirit" is derived from the prominent place which he occupies in Acts. While he recognizes this place, Frank Stagg points out that the purpose of Acts is not to present such a Gospel.[1] He points out that after 21:11, except for 28:25 where the Spirit is cited in connection with prophecy, the Holy Spirit is not mentioned in Acts. This is true. Yet, in the light of preceding passages, one cannot fail to see the work of the Holy Spirit in the remainder. Of course, Stagg most likely would agree with this statement. And even though, as he says, prominent mention is made in Acts concerning God, the angel of the Lord, and "the Lord," we cannot isolate the Holy Spirit from these references. As, in the remainder of the Bible, certain personalities of deity are mentioned—sometimes separate, sometimes identical—the same may be said of Acts.

We are not contending that Luke's purpose in Acts was to write a "gospel of the Holy Spirit." There are many secondary purposes found in the book. However, we like Stagg's idea that the overriding purpose was to record how the gospel overcame various prejudices as it spread throughout the Roman world, finally to arrive at the place where it might be preached "unhinderedly" (*akōlupōs,* adverb, the last word in Acts, Nestle's text). But all of this was accomplished through the power of the Holy Spirit.

Pentecost marks a signal point in the economy of God. The day of Pentecost came fifty days after the Passover. It was the feast which commemorated the end of the grain harvest. Thus it was one of the more important feasts of the Jews and was characterized by great rejoicing.

But the Christian significance stems from the fact that on that day the Holy Spirit came upon the followers of Jesus in a special manifestation. Certainly this did not mark the entrance of the Holy Spirit into the affairs of history, for he had been active from the beginning, as we have seen in previous discussions. But it does mark a new departure in God's eternal redemptive purpose. For the Spirit of God came upon the Christian community, empowered it, and gave to it a *fellowship (koinōnia) in the Holy Spirit,* and sent it forth to proclaim God's redemptive work in Christ to a lost world. It is significant to note that after Acts 2 this day in the Christian sense is not mentioned in the New Testament. The emphasis was always upon the crucifixion and resurrection. But one cannot escape the fact that the proclamation in power of these mighty events followed the Pentecost experience (cf. Acts 2:23–24). The Holy Spirit took the things of Christ, and through his followers proclaimed them to men.

"When the day of Pentecost was fully come, they were all with one accord [together] in one place" (Acts 2:1). Where this place was is not stated. G. Campbell Morgan sees it as the Temple, since it was here that the celebration of Pentecost centered.[2] However, the tone of the account suggests that the disciples were elsewhere, sitting in a house (v.2). This suggests the house of the "upper room" (1:13), perhaps the home of Mary, the mother of John Mark (12:12). It could be, however, that after the Spirit came upon them, the disciples went to the Temple to proclaim the fact.

Wherever it took place, the event was phenomenal. "Suddenly there came a sound from heaven as of a rushing mighty wind" (2:2). The Spirit himself did not come in the *form* of wind, but with a *sound* as of a tornado, a sound which filled the house. Then there appeared "cloven tongues like as of fire, and it sat upon each of them" (v.3).

To the audible sign was added a visible one. This visible sign was not fire; it was "as if" (*hōsei*) fire or it looked like fire. The "tongues" themselves were not "cloven." This sign appeared as one body. Then suddenly it parted in this direction and that, resting distributively on each disciple. "These audible and visible signs were but passing phenomena; the presence and power of the Holy Spirit was the permanent and important reality." [3]

However, these signs are not without meaning. *Pnoē* (wind) is akin to *pneuma* (wind, spirit). To the Jews, fire had always been a symbol of the divine presence (Ex. 3:2; Deut. 5:4). John the Baptist had said that the Christ would baptize in the Holy Spirit and in fire (Matt. 3:11). Furthermore, wind and fire are basic elements of power in nature.

It is of interest to note the contrast between the Son's coming into the world for his ministry and the Spirit's coming for his. As the Suffering Servant, Jesus at Bethlehem almost *slipped* into the world, largely unnoticed by men. But the Holy Spirit, the power of Jehovah, came at Pentecost in the midst of the phenomena commensurate to his nature. Thereafter, each proceeded to do his work in keeping with the Father's will.

What was the immediate effect of the coming of the Spirit

upon the disciples? "They were all filled with the Holy Ghost
[Spirit], and began to speak with other tongues, as the Spirit
gave them utterance" (Acts 2:4). "Tongues" (*glōssais*) means
"languages." We still speak of the mother tongue or the English
tongue. So these were intelligible languages. "Other" (*heterais*)
means *others of a different kind*. Therefore, these were languages
other than the native ones of the speakers. And they spoke them
as the Spirit gave them utterance.

Why this phenomenon? Soon a crowd gathered, a crowd composed of Palestinian Jews and of people from fifteen different parts
of the world other than Palestine (vv.9–11). Most of these were
"Jews, devout men, out of every nation under heaven" (v.5).
They were Jews of the Dispersion. But there were also some
Gentile proselytes who were Gentiles by birth. These Jews of the
Dispersion may or may not have been able to speak Aramaic,
the current Jewish tongue. The Hebrew Scriptures had been translated into Greek (Septuagint) because so many of the Dispersion
had forgotten how to speak their native tongue. But even if it be
assumed that the Jews of the Dispersion who were present could
speak Aramaic, the phenomenon still remains. For as each of
them heard these Spirit-filled disciples speak, he heard in his
own tongue (vv.7–8). Here the word "tongue" is "dialect"
(*dialektos*). Each heard not only in the language of his native
land, but in his own peculiar dialect of that language.

They heard "the wonderful [mighty] works of God" (v.11).
So this was not mere jargon which they heard. These disciples
were declaring what God had wrought, not only the giving of the
Spirit but also of salvation through Jesus Christ. They were
preaching the gospel in languages other than their own. Was this
a miracle of speaking, or hearing, or both? Probably the last.
The point is that the disciples were enabled to preach the gospel
so as to be understood by those who spoke a foreign tongue.
This is one explanation of the rapid spread of the gospel through-

out the Roman world. Foakes-Jackson suggests that this miracle of languages at Pentecost was "symbolical of the coming universality of the gospel." [4] Whether or not this was its intent, it certainly fits the case.

Robertson calls attention to the three miracles of Pentecost: sound, tongues like fire, and untaught languages. "But one is not to confound these miraculous signs with the Holy Spirit. They are merely proof that he has come to carry on the work of his dispensation." [5] The first two signs disappeared immediately. The last one appears for some time, but it also was to cease (cf. 1 Cor. 13:8).[6]

Some of these who witnessed this miracle of languages mocked, saying that these Christians were drunk. But in response Peter preached one of his greatest sermons, declaring this to be the fulfilment of the prophecy of Joel 2:28–32 (cf. Acts 2:14 ff.). Then he preached concerning the crucifixion and resurrection of Jesus. The phenomena at Pentecost gave place to the preaching at Pentecost. The Holy Spirit does not call attention to himself. He exalts Christ. The results at Pentecost attest to his work and his power (2:41).

Events moved rapidly following Pentecost. To the three thousand believers won on that day soon there were added five thousand others (4:4). The success of this movement soon brought on persecution by the Sadducees (vv.1 ff.). But the Holy Spirit encouraged and sustained the Christians in it (v.31). The fellowship brought about through the Spirit expressed itself in a great wave of sharing (2:44–45; 4:34 ff.). Those who had possessions sold them to provide for the needs of those who probably had lost their livelihood in the persecution. This practice was not a germ of communism. It was Christian fellowship (*koinōnia*) in action.

Out of this experience comes a distinct reference to the personality of the Holy Spirit. In keeping with the example of others,

Ananias and his wife, Sapphira, sold a possession. But while claiming to give all of the proceeds to the fund of sharing, they actually gave only a portion and kept the rest for themselves. They sought credit without paying the price. That this was not communism is seen in the fact that it was a voluntary matter (5:4). Knowing of their deceitful act, Peter accused Ananias of *lying to the Holy Spirit* (5:3).

Stagg suggests as a possible translation "to falsify the Holy Spirit." Thus the charge is even more than lying to the Holy Spirit. "He falsified the Spirit as he sought to represent his fraudulent deed as something inspired by the Spirit. Thus he tried to make the Spirit a party to his own crime." [7] Ananias died suddenly, and later the same fate befell his wife. It is no wonder that "great fear came upon all the church, and upon as many as heard these things" (5:11). The Holy Spirit is a helper to the faithful, but he is not to be trifled with.

Even among the faithful of the fellowship there arose a problem. In the distribution of the funds which were provided, a charge of discrimination was made. The Grecian Jews, or those from outside Palestine, charged against the Palestinian Jews that their widows were being neglected in the daily ministration (6:1). These were Jews who had become Christians.

The apostles called the believers together, saying, "It is not reason that we should leave the word of God, and serve tables" (6:2). Therefore, they requested the church to select seven men (note that they did not do this themselves) whom they would appoint over the business of ministrations. One of the qualifications was that they should be men "full of the Holy Ghost [Spirit]" (v.3). While the office is not named, this probably is the origin of the office of deacon. The result of this new arrangement was that "the word of God increased [was preached and taught more abundantly]; and the number of the disciples multiplied in Jerusalem greatly" (6:7).

But the office of deacon was not limited to the serving of tables. For one of the seven, Stephen, "full of faith and power, did great wonders and miracles among the people" (6:8). This was the work of the Holy Spirit through him. And it soon led him into conflict with certain Jews. He was brought before the "council" or the Sanhedrin (*sunedrion*). Wild charges were made against him, including blasphemy against Moses, the Temple, and God.

When the high priest asked if these things were true, Stephen delivered a masterful address. He closed by charging, "Ye stiff-necked and uncircumcised in heart and ears, ye do always resist the Holy Ghost [Spirit]: as your fathers did, so do ye" (7:51).

This charge largely encompassed the whole of Israel's history up until then. This was more than they could take. So "they gnashed on him with their teeth" (v.54).

But Stephen, "being full of the Holy Ghost [Spirit], looked up stedfastly into heaven, and saw the glory of God, and Jesus standing on the right hand of God, and said, Behold, I see the heavens opened" (7:55–56).

This was more than the Sanhedrin could stand. So they cried out in horror, stopped their ears so as not to hear further, cast Stephen out of the city, and stoned him to death. Stephen, meanwhile, prayed, "Lord Jesus, receive my spirit. And he kneeled down, and cried with a loud voice, Lord, lay not this sin to their charge. And when he had said this, he fell asleep" (7:59–60). Thus the Holy Spirit sustained him as he became the first believer to pay for his faith with his life.

Those who stoned Stephen laid their clothes at the feet of a young rabbi named Saul. Since he cast no stones, evidently he was not one of the accusers. But he saw Stephen die. And the Holy Spirit never let him forget the sight. Its memory prepared him for his experience with Jesus on the Damascus road (9:5). Truly, the blood of the martyrs is the seed of the church!

The death of Stephen set off a wave of persecution against the

Christians (8:1). Apparently Saul of Tarsus was the leader of this persecution (v.3). The result was that for the first time after Pentecost the Christian community was scattered beyond Jerusalem. "Therefore, they that were scattered abroad went every where preaching the word" (v.4). This marked the beginning of the spread of the gospel throughout the Roman world. And as will be seen at a later time, the Holy Spirit was involved in each new development in this vast enterprise.[8]

One other matter calls for attention in regard to the Holy Spirit in Acts—the receiving of the Holy Spirit. In Acts 2:38, Peter exhorted his listeners to "repent, and be baptized every one of you in the name of Jesus Christ for [eis, on the basis of, as the result of] the remission of sins, and ye shall receive the . . . Holy Ghost [Spirit]." Jesus had said that the Holy Spirit would indwell every believer (John 14:17). So we may understand Peter's promise in this light.

Throughout the book of Acts there are significant occasions in which the Holy Spirit came upon believers after Pentecost. We shall have occasion to examine these again in chapter 8. Our present purpose is to scan these with regard to the method of receiving the Spirit and its significance for the individual believer. Of interest is the fact that this receiving was not a "second blessing." For in Acts, except where the Spirit came upon or manifested himself to the church, every other instance is in connection with conversion.

For example, when Philip preached in Samaria many people believed and were baptized. But they had not yet received the Holy Spirit (8:16). Peter and John, two apostles, were sent down from Jerusalem. Upon arrival they "prayed for them, that they might receive the Holy Ghost [Spirit]" (v.15). "Then laid they their hands on them, and they received the Holy Ghost [Spirit]" (v.17).

Some infer from this a procedure by which one receives the

Holy Spirit; namely baptism, prayer, the laying on of hands, and that at the hands of an apostle. But such an inference leads into difficulties. Saul of Tarsus (Paul) received the Holy Spirit with no mention of prayer, before baptism, and at the laying on of the hands of Ananias, a simple disciple—not an apostle, not even a deacon. The converted disciples of John the Baptist received the Spirit, without prayer, but at the laying on of the hands of the apostle Paul (19:6). The Holy Spirit came upon those converted in the house of Cornelius without prayer, before baptism, and without the laying on of hands, even while Peter was still preaching (10:44).

The point of all this is that the Holy Spirit does not work by any one preconceived system. Morgan is very clear at this point:

The moment that we become mystified in the presence of the operations of the Spirit, we have reached the heart of truth. "The wind bloweth where it will, and thou hearest the voice thereof, but knowest not whence it cometh, and whither it goeth." The moment in which any theologian, or school of theology, attempts to systematize the method of the coming of the Spirit into human lives, in that moment they are excluding a score of His operations, and including only one . . . "The wind bloweth where it will"; and this is the supreme glory of the Christian Church. Its life and its power is not that of organization or ministry, but that of the indwelling Spirit.[9]

One thing is clear. In keeping with Jesus' promise, the Holy Spirit comes upon the individual in connection with the conversion experience, and not as a "second blessing." A good example of this is seen in connection with the disciples of John the Baptist in Ephesus. Paul asked them, "Have ye received the Holy Ghost [Spirit] since ye believed?" (Acts 19:2). The King James Version could mean a "second blessing" subsequent to conversion. But a literal reading is, "If the Holy Spirit you received believing." Or better still, "Did you receive the Holy Spirit when you believed?" These disciples of John replied that they knew nothing of the

Holy Spirit having been given. It evolved that they knew only the baptism of John. They were unaware of the atoning work of Christ. But when they heard from Paul about Christ Jesus, "they were baptized in the name of the Lord Jesus," which implies their faith in him. It was then that they received the Holy Spirit, not *since* they believed but *when* they believed (19:5).

What is the significance of the coming of the Holy Spirit upon the believers? In 1 Corinthians 12:13, Paul says, "By one Spirit are we all baptized into one body"—the body of Christ. The moment, therefore, that one believes in Jesus he is baptized of the Holy Spirit into the body of Christ, the fellowship or *koinōnia* of believers.

Along with many other significant facts, this is one of the great doctrines of the Holy Spirit taught in the book of Acts.

The Pauline Epistles

Paul is quite clear in his treatment of the Holy Spirit as a distinct person of the Godhead. This distinction is sharply defined in his benediction in 2 Corinthians 13:14. Here he speaks of "the grace of the Lord Jesus Christ, the love of God, and the communion of the Holy Ghost [Spirit]." This distinction is further emphasized by the words grace, love, and communion—elements relating to these distinct persons of the Godhead respectively. In Ephesians 4:4–6, the apostle speaks of "one Spirit, one Lord [Christ]," and "one God and Father." In 1 Corinthians 2:11, he distinguishes between "God" and "the Spirit of God."

However, at other times Paul speaks of the Holy Spirit as related to, and at times identical with, the other persons of deity. In one verse he notes the intermingling of all three persons of the Godhead: "Ye are not in the flesh, but in the Spirit, if so be that the Spirit of God dwell in you. Now if any man have not the Spirit of Christ, he is none of his" (Rom. 8:9; cf. 8:11; 1 Cor. 12:3). Here then Paul speaks of the Holy Spirit as the Spirit of both God and Christ. This same relationship, though not so clearly stated, appears also in Romans 8:14–17.

Furthermore, in Galatians 4:6, Paul speaks of the Spirit of God's Son. And in 1 Corinthians 15:45, Christ, or the second Adam, is called a quickening or life-giving Spirit. Second Corinthians 3:17 reads, "Now the Lord is that Spirit: and where the Spirit of the Lord is, there is liberty."

Paul recognizes the distinct personality of the Holy Spirit. As in other biblical references he is the Spirit sent forth from God to do his work. Yet at times he identifies the Holy Spirit and Christ, not in the sense that they are not distinct persons, but that they are distinct persons doing identical work. So to be "in Christ" is to be in the Spirit or to have the Spirit in you, and to be thus in the Spirit is to be "in Christ." Mullins notes that "their task and aim being identical, there was no discord in Paul's mind in explaining their activities in similar terms." [10]

Paul is at one with Jesus in noting that as a person the Holy Spirit indwells every believer. "The love of God is shed abroad in our hearts by the Holy Ghost [Spirit] which is given unto us" (Rom. 5:5). The law of the Spirit of life in Christ Jesus frees the believer from the law of sin and death (Rom. 8:2). Indeed, if one is not indwelt by the Spirit he does not belong to Christ (Rom. 8:9–11).

Spiritual cleansing, sanctification, and justification are wrought in the believer in the name of the Lord Jesus Christ and in the Spirit of God (1 Cor. 6:11; cf. Titus 3:5). The believer is sealed by the Spirit who also is his guarantee of salvation (2 Cor. 1:22; 5:5; Eph. 1:13). Paul challenges the Galatian Christians to consider the place of faith and/or works in their Christian experience (3:2–3). Since they received the Holy Spirit through faith, not works, they should continue to grow in that experience in the Spirit, and not by the works of the flesh. The apostle himself recognized that his "preaching was not with enticing words of man's wisdom, but in demonstration of the Spirit and of power" (1 Cor. 2:4).

The strongest statement made by Paul regarding the Holy Spirit in the believer is found in 1 Corinthians 6:19-20: "Know ye not that your body is the temple of the Holy Ghost [Spirit] which is in you, which ye have of God, and ye are not your own? For ye are bought with a price: therefore glorify God in your body." Literally, "Do you not know that your body is a temple of the Holy Spirit in you?" (cf. 1 Cor. 3:16).

The word "temple" renders a Greek word *naos*. This word was used for the holy of holies in the Jewish temple. In this *naos* God was said to dwell with his people in mercy. Into it only the high priest might enter once each year on the Day of Atonement. It was the veil of this *naos* that was torn asunder when Jesus died on Calvary, signifying that in Christ man had unhindered access to God (cf. Heb. 4:16).

But Paul says even more. He says that in Christ, God in the Holy Spirit actually dwells in the believer who is now the *naos* of God. The spirit of man indwells man, and the Holy Spirit indwells the believer's spirit. The Greek text has no definite article before *naos*. So the believer is not "the temple" of the Holy Spirit, as though he were confined to the believer. Since the Holy Spirit is omnipresent this would not be possible, even as the *naos* in Jerusalem could not contain Jehovah. But each believer is a *naos* of the Holy Spirit. While he is elsewhere and works as he wills, he still is in the Christian and chooses to work through him.

This thought carries tremendous meaning. As a purchased possession of God you belong to him; he has purchased his dwelling place. And since you belong to him, you should glorify him in your body. The King James Version adds "and in your spirit, which are God's" (1 Cor. 6:20). But the best manuscripts end with "glorify God in your body." Some later scribe probably added to this to soften what is a striking thought of Paul. The body is not essentially evil; it is the sanctuary of God. And you can glorify God in and through a body dedicated to God through the Holy Spirit.

One further matter remains for our present treatment, and that is the Holy Spirit in the church. As the Spirit indwells the individual believer, even so he also indwells the church, the company of believers.

Writing to the church in Corinth Paul says, "Know ye not that ye are the temple [*naos*] of God, and that the Spirit of God dwelleth in you? If any man defile [destroy] the temple of God, him shall God destroy [same word as for defile]; for the temple [*naos*] of God is holy, which temple ye are" (1 Cor. 3:16–17). So even as the body of each believer is indwelt by the Spirit, also the body of believers is indwelt by him.

In the case of the individual believer the emphasis is placed upon his own body which is subject to being abused in fleshly sins. But in the case of the body of believers, Paul's emphasis is upon harmony within that composite body. Through strife within the church the members were creating a schism (1 Cor. 3:3 ff.), thus threatening to destroy that body. Paul warns that if one destroys this body, God will destroy him. This should give caution to any person tempted to disrupt the fellowship of any church. In Ephesians 4:3, Paul exhorts us "to keep the unity of the Spirit in the bond of peace."

It is in light of the Spirit's indwelling the church that we can best understand the "fellowship" or *koinōnia* of the church. This is one of the great words used in the New Testament for the Christian relationship in the church. It has a variety of meanings: association, communion, fellowship, close relationship, generosity, fellow feeling, brotherly unity, participation, and sharing. To destroy any of these is to injure or destroy the *koinōnia*. Thus we can understand Paul's warning in 1 Corinthians 3:17.

Christ calls us into this relationship (1 Cor. 1:9). And it is effected and perfected by the Holy Spirit (2 Cor. 3:3; 13:14; Phil. 2:1). Without using the word, Paul relates in Ephesians 2:14–22 how this *koinōnia* is effected. Both Jews and Gentiles are made one in Christ. Christ is the chief cornerstone "in whom all the building fitly framed together groweth unto an holy temple [*naos*] in the Lord: In whom ye also are builded together for an habitation of God through the Spirit."

Employing the figure of the human body the apostle expresses the same idea in more detail (1 Cor. 12).[11] Here he pictures the various members of the body of Christ as interrelated and endowed by the Holy Spirit for service. "Now there are diversities of gifts, but the same Spirit" (1 Cor. 12:4; cf. vv.7 ff.). "For by one Spirit are we all baptized into one body, whether we be Jews or Gentiles, whether we be bond or free; and have been all made to drink into one Spirit" (v.13).

So Paul sees the Spirit of God as a person glorifying Christ, and his work, as he operates in and through believers individually and collectively, edifying the church, preserving its fellowship, and empowering it for service. We may well sum up the matter by citing his words to the church in Corinth: "Forasmuch as ye are manifestly declared to be the epistle of Christ ministered by us, written not with ink, but with the Spirit of the living God; not in tables of stone, but in fleshy tables of the heart" (2 Cor. 3:3).

The General Epistles and Revelation

There is little new to add to this general survey as found in this section of the New Testament. But a few matters are worthy of note.

In Hebrews we find a reference to the gifts of the Holy Spirit (2:4). The Spirit is mentioned as inspiring the Old Testament Scriptures (3:7; 9:8; 10:15). Mention has been made previously of Christ's going to the cross in the "eternal Spirit" (9:14). Christians are called "partakers of [partners with] the Holy Ghost [Spirit]" (6:4). In Hebrews 4:12–13, the "word of God" is used in a personal sense as a sharp, two-edged sword, which is suggestive of Paul's word about "the sword of the Spirit, which is the word of God" (Eph. 6:17).

The epistles of Peter also take note of the Holy Spirit. He is described as resting upon believers (1 Peter 4:14). He is noted also as the one inspiring writers of the Scriptures (2 Peter 1:21; cf. 1 Peter 1:11–12).

First John 3:24 gives the presence of the Spirit as evidence that one is a Christian. It is by the Spirit that one confesses that Jesus Christ is come in the flesh (4:2–3). First John 5:6–8 lists the Trinity, and points out the Spirit as bearing witness to Christ. Here he says that "the Spirit is truth." And in verse 16, while not mentioning the Holy Spirit, he speaks of the "sin unto death," which sounds ominously like the sin against the Holy Spirit.

Jude's one mention of the Holy Spirit speaks of "praying in the Holy Ghost [Spirit]" (v. 20). This is akin to Paul's "praying always with all prayer and supplication in the Spirit" (Eph. 6:18).

Revelation repeatedly mentions the Holy Spirit. Its visions were given to John while he was "in the Spirit on the Lord's day" (1:10; cf. 4:2). Through him the Spirit speaks to the seven churches of Asia Minor (2:7,11,29; 3:6,13,22). Nowhere else in the New Testament does the Spirit give a greater picture of the glorified, triumphant Christ.

Revelation gives a fitting close to the entire canon, as it pictures the Holy Spirit along with the church, the bride of Christ, calling to a lost world. "The Spirit and the bride say, Come. And let him that heareth say, Come. And let him that is athirst come. And whosoever will, let him take the water of life freely" (22:17).

The Written Record
5

The Bible is the written record of God's revelation to men concerning his person, will, work, and purposes. It is well at the outset to set forth a statement of faith concerning the Bible.

"The Holy Bible was written by men divinely inspired and is the record of God's revelation of Himself to man. It is a perfect treasure of divine instruction. It has God for its author, salvation for its end, and truth, without any mixture of error, for its matter. It reveals the principles by which God judges us; and therefore is, and will remain to the end of the world, the true center of Christian union, and the supreme standard by which all human conduct, creeds, and religious opinions should be tried. The criterion by which the Bible is to be interpreted is Jesus Christ." [1]

The purpose of this chapter is to study the place of the Holy Spirit in bringing the Bible into being (cf. 2 Tim. 3:16; 2 Peter 1:21; 3:2). For this purpose it is necessary to consider three terms: revelation, illumination, and inspiration.

Revealed

Revelation is the process by which God unveils himself and his will to human messengers. The Greek word is *apokalupsis,* meaning an uncovering (Rom. 2:5; 1 Cor. 14:6; Gal. 1:12; Eph. 3:3; Rev. 1:1).

God reveals himself in nature. In this sense all men have a

revelation of God. "Because that which may be known of God is manifest in [to] them; for God hath shewed it unto them. For the invisible things of him from the creation of the world are clearly seen, being understood by the things that are made, even his eternal power and Godhead [*theiotēs,* Godhood or divinity]; so that they are without excuse" (Rom. 1:19–20; cf. Psalm 19:1).

At this point it is well to distinguish between revelation and discovery. Revelation is the self-uncovering of God. In this act God is both *subject* and *object.* He is subject in that he *reveals.* He is object in that he reveals *himself.* And man is the *recipient* of the revelation. Discovery, on the other hand, is an effort on man's part to find God. In this process man is the subject in that he searches. God is the object of man's search. The method of man's search is reason. Romans 1:21 ff. declares the result of such a search. Rejecting God's revelation in nature, he sought to discover God through reason. The result was polytheism. He made many gods, but he did not discover the true God. Paganism is the fruit of man's search through reason. The religion of Jehovah is the fruit of God's revelation of himself.

Revelation in the biblical sense involves a personal unveiling of God in terms of moral and spiritual principles to and through human messengers (Gen. 12:1; Ex. 20:1; Isa. 6:1–8; Rev. 1:1). The author of Hebrews sums up this truth. "God, who at sundry times and in divers manners [many measures and many manners or ways] spake in time past unto the fathers by [*en,* in] the prophets, hath in these last days spoken unto us by his Son [*en huiōi,* in a Son, or one who bore the relation of Son]" (1:1–2). So through the centuries God revealed himself by "various measures" and "various manners" [2] in the prophets. But in the "last of these days" he revealed himself supremely in his Son, Jesus Christ.

Already in our study we have noted the role of the Holy Spirit as one sent forth from God to do his specific work. And this work has to do with the revelation of God. For God reveals himself in his mighty acts through nature, history, and men. He reveals himself through his Law, and through the moral and spiritual principles enunciated by the prophets. His supreme revelation is in Jesus Christ.

It is not always necessary for the Spirit to be mentioned by name for us to see his activity. One cannot read the prophets without being conscious of the fact that they declare a message which was not their own. There is a God-consciousness about them which speaks of the unveiling of the divine. Jeremiah's awareness of a prenatal call (1:4–5); Isaiah's signal experience in the Temple (6:1–8); "the beginning of the word of the Lord by Hosea" (1:2); and "the word of the Lord that came to Joel" (1:1)—all declare that here were men who had received a divine vision and message. Ezekiel's experience may be said to be dramatically the experience of all. "He said unto me, Son of man, stand upon thy feet, and I will speak unto thee. And the spirit entered into me when he spake unto me, and set me upon my feet, that I heard him that spake unto me" (2:1–2). It is no wonder that their messages bristled with, "Thus saith the Lord." It was the Lord Jehovah speaking through his Spirit.

This Peter declares when he speaks of the prophets "who prophesied of the grace that should come unto you . . . or what manner of time the Spirit of Christ which was in them did signify, when it [he] testified beforehand the sufferings of Christ, and the glory that should follow" (1 Peter 1:10–11).

How else could David in Psalm 22 set forth the grim details of the crucifixion? How else could Isaiah 53, more than seven hundred years before the event, depict so eloquently the earthly life of Jesus from his youth through the resurrection and beyond? How else could he portray the Suffering Servant in such fashion that Isaiah 53:4–9 may well be called the "Good Friday of the Old Testament?" It was the Holy Spirit speaking to and through the consciousness of men who wrote more than their natural minds could know. God sent forth his Spirit to reveal prophetically his great love toward all men as expressed through his Son.

As the author of Hebrews reminds us, the climax of God's revelation came in Jesus Christ. John 1:17 says, "The law was given by [through] Moses, but grace and truth came [became, came into being] by [through] Jesus Christ." When God would reveal his law, he did so through a man. But when he revealed his grace and truth, he himself became flesh and blood (cf. John 1:1,14). From beginning to end this involved a vital work of the Holy Spirit.

Recall the survey of the Holy Spirit in the Gospels. Jesus was conceived by the Holy Spirit. By him he was anointed. He wrought and taught by the Holy Spirit (Luke 4:14–21). He went to the cross in the Holy Spirit, and God raised him from the dead "according to the spirit of holiness" (Rom. 1:4; cf. Heb. 9:14).

John 1:14, in one parenthetical phrase, runs the gamut of the entire revelation of God in Jesus Christ: "We beheld his glory, the glory as of the only begotten of the Father." This beholding is not limited to the transfiguration but encompasses the whole of Jesus' public ministry (cf. 1 John 1:1–3). In his Word, God through the Holy Spirit unveiled the heart and mind of the Father as grace and truth—when God became Jesus of Nazareth!

Beyond the Gospels the revelation of God through the Holy Spirit continued. The coming of the Spirit at Pentecost was itself a revelation of God's moral and spiritual power. In the Holy Spirit, Stephen was given a revelation of the glorified Christ in heaven (Acts 7:55–56). Saul's vision of the risen Jesus on the Damascus road was a revelation (Acts 9:3 ff.).

While at times Paul made direct reference to teachings of Jesus while on earth, he repeatedly made claim to direct revelation. He insisted that the gospel which he preached was not received by him through man's communication: "I neither received it of man, neither was I taught it, but by the revelation of Jesus

Christ" (Gal. 1:12). Introducing his account of the Lord's Supper, he said, "I have received of the Lord that which also I delivered unto you" (1 Cor. 11:23). He makes the same claim with regard to the basic elements of the gospel (1 Cor. 15:3 ff.).

In Ephesians 3, the apostle expounds the "mystery of Christ" that the Gentiles, along with the Jews, "should be fellowheirs, and of the same body, and partakers of his promise in Christ" (v.6). He begins this exposition with the words, "How that by revelation he [God] made known unto me the mystery" (v.3). And this revelation he attributes to "the Spirit" (v.5).

Paul's words in 1 Corinthians 15:27–28 could have come only by direct revelation. For there is no other mention of such anywhere else in the Bible, not even from Jesus himself. All other references to the ultimate in eschatology end with the judgment —Christ, having subdued all things under himself, reigns supreme. But Paul looks beyond that to see even the Son subject to the Father, "that God may be all in all" (v.28). In a completely re-deemed and subdued universe, both naturally and spiritually, the Father, Son, and Holy Spirit will be seen as God. We shall see him as he is, "that God may be all in all." (The wicked are in hell, of course, but that is secondary in Paul's present thinking.)

Paul's clearest claim to revelation, and one which explains the whole, is found in 2 Corinthians 12. Exactly when and where this experience occurred is a mystery. It may have happened in his sojourn in "Arabia," whatever he means by this, shortly after his conversion (Gal. 1:17). Or it could have been later at Tarsus (Acts 9:30; 11:25). But wherever it happened, he says, "I will come to visions and revelations of the Lord" (v.1). Then he sets forth an experience so intimate that he describes it as though it happened to another. Whether in the body or out of the body he was "caught up to [in] the third heaven . . . into paradise" (vv. 2–4).

Alfred Plummer notes that by the "third heaven" he means the highest heaven where God is. Here he "heard unspeakable [inexpressible] words, which it is not lawful for a man to utter" (v.4). He was forbidden to put them into human language even had he been able to do so. However, his repeated references to speaking by revelation suggest that much that he heard he could speak.

So great was this experience that, to guard him from inordinate pride, he was given a "thorn in the flesh" (whatever it was, v.7). Three times Paul prayed for its removal. But God said, "My grace is sufficient for thee: for my strength is made perfect in weakness" (v.9). Then gladly the apostle accepted it, "that the *power* [Holy Spirit] of Christ may rest upon me" (v.9).

Now this was obviously a supernatural experience. And our knowledge of God's work through his Holy Spirit naturally leads us to attribute it to him.

Space forbids an exhaustive treatment of the work of the Holy Spirit in revelation. But said treatment would be incomplete, indeed, without a glance at Revelation.

"The Revelation of Jesus Christ, which God gave unto him, to shew unto his servants things which must shortly come to pass; and he sent and signified [sign-i-fied] it by his angel unto his servant John" (Rev. 1:1).

Thus begins this awesome but beautiful book in which the living Christ admonishes and encourages the churches of Asia Minor, following which there emerges scene after scene in the divine drama wherein is portrayed the glorified Christ in triumph over his foes, judging and punishing Satan and all who are his, rewarding the faithful, after which time blends into the ever unfolding and limitless glory of eternity.

How did John see all of this? By revelation through the Holy Spirit. For he said, "I was in the Spirit on the Lord's day" (Rev. 1:10).

Illumined

Illumination is the act of God whereby the human messenger is given the spiritual insight necessary to understand that which is revealed (cf. Eph. 1:18; Heb. 10:32). It was through this divinely given perception that the writers in the Bible could understand the moving tides of history. Thus Moses saw the journey of Abraham from Ur of the Chaldees to Palestine as more than the mere migration of a nomadic people. It was the mighty movement of God as he set in motion his eternal redemptive purpose.

The exodus of Israel from Egypt was not simply the escape of a long-enslaved people. It was a mighty deliverance of God as he led a prepared nation toward a prepared purpose. To the prophets the swirling tides of history in their times were more than political intrigue, war, and captivity. They saw God working through it all to purify a rebellious people and to call them back to their God-given destiny.

Through illumination, Paul looked beyond the wars of Greece and Rome and the stagnation of the waters of religion to see "the fulness of the time" when "God sent forth his Son" (Gal. 4:4) to be the Redeemer of a lost and dismal race. Likewise, John on Patmos could see beyond the terrible persecution of the Christians in Asia Minor to the full and final victory of Christ over his enemies and those of his people.

In illumination God is the subject and man is the object. God illumines; man is illumined. Electricity is light; a bulb is illumined as the electricity flows through it. So the Holy Spirit is God's Spirit sent forth to perform through illumination in the minds of men. Thus God enables men to understand his revelation of himself. The work of the Holy Spirit in revelation and inspiration in the scriptural sense ended with the New Testament. But his work in illumination continues as he enables Spirit-filled men to understand and interpret the Bible, God's inspired, written revelation.

However, our concern at this point is the work of the Holy Spirit as he illumined the minds of those who received and recorded God's revelation. Already we have seen how through illumination men were enabled to interpret history in terms of God's redemptive purpose. But to illustrate this work of the Holy Spirit further, we shall note three other evidences of illumination.

The first of these is the Spirit's work in enabling the writer of Hebrews to understand the ultimate meaning of Levitical law. Three times in his letter he cites the Holy Spirit as inspiring the Old Testament Scriptures (3:7; 9:8; 10:15). But he also says that God's complete revelation was in his Son (1:2). It is natural, therefore, that Hebrews should center in Christ as the fulfilment of these Old Testament Scriptures. One of his major emphases centers in the Levitical law. Beginning with the Old Testament elements, in each case he shows how they find their true fulfilment in Christ and his redemptive work.

Naturally the author begins this interpretation by comparing the high priesthood of Jesus with that of Aaron (4:14 to 7:28). Whereas the Aaronic priesthood was temporary, that of Christ is eternal. Likening Jesus' priesthood to that of Melchizedek (5:10 ff.), he points out that in every respect it is superior to that of Aaron. Furthermore, Christ is the minister of a better covenant with better promises than that of Aaron (chap. 8). This new covenant is the fulfilment of Jehovah's promise revealed in Jeremiah 31:31-34. Again, Jesus ministers in a better sanctuary than that of Aaron (9:1-12). Aaron's tabernacle was earthly; Jesus' sanctuary is heavenly. It naturally follows, therefore, that Jesus offers a better sacrifice (9:13 to 10:18). Indeed, he is both priest, sacrifice, and Lord. "Neither by the blood of goats and calves, but by his own blood he entered in once [*ephapax,* once for all] into the holy place, having obtained eternal redemption for us" (9:12). "Christ is not entered into the holy places made with hands, which are the figures of the true; but into heaven itself, now to appear in the presence of God for us: . . . now once [*hapax*] in the end of the world hath he appeared to put away sin by the sacrifice of himself. . . . after he had offered one sacrifice for sins for ever, [he] sat down on the right hand of God; from henceforth expecting till his enemies be made his footstool" (9:24 to 10:13).

That which in the Old Testament the Spirit had given in a "pattern" (9:24, ASV), through the writer of Hebrews he interprets as the "true." This he did through illumination.

The second such work we would cite is an understanding of the fulfilment of prophecy. One striking example of this is Peter, filled with the Holy Spirit, interpreting the coming of the Spirit at Pentecost as the fulfilment of Joel 2:28–32 (Acts 2:16 ff.).

Paul saw the refusal of the gospel by Jews in Rome as a fulfilment of Isaiah 6:9–10 (Acts 28:24 ff.; cf. Matt. 13:14). A reading of the writings of Paul reveals his abundance of interpretations of Old Testament prophecies. In lesser degree this is true of many other New Testament writings.

An analysis of the four Gospels is most revealing. Matthew has forty-six passages in which he records the interpretation of sixty-six prophecies. Mark has twenty-one passages in which he records the interpretation of twenty-six prophecies. In Luke there are thirty-five passages interpreting fifty-two prophecies. In John twelve passages interpret thirteen prophecies. Of course, many of these are interpreted by Jesus himself. But even the human mind of Jesus was enlightened by the Holy Spirit, though to a degree beyond that of any other person.

The third area of illumination under present consideration is with regard to the disciples' remembrance of things taught them by Jesus, and the further teaching by the Holy Spirit. On the night before his death, Jesus said to his apostles, "I have yet many things to say unto you, but ye cannot bear them now. Howbeit when he, the Spirit of truth, is come, he will guide you into all truth . . . and he will shew you things to come" (John 16:12–13). Shortly before this he had said that the Holy Spirit would "teach you all things, and bring all things to your remembrance, whatsoever I have said unto you" (John 14:26).

For three and one-half years Jesus had taught. During most of this time these men had sat at the feet of the greatest of all teachers. It was almost like sitting in a continuous seminar listening to him who is Truth itself. Hardly knowing it, their subconsciousness was a crowded storehouse of wisdom. The Gospels themselves speak of their ability to remember. Of course, through centuries of training and practice the Jews had developed tremendous memories and the ability of recall. But even this does not explain the memory and recall of these men. Jesus explained it when he said that the Holy Spirit shall "bring all things to your remembrance, whatsoever I have said unto you."

So greatly was this promise fulfilled that John closes his Gospel, which abounds with evidence of his remembrance, with these words: "There are also many other things which Jesus did, the which, if they should be written every one, I suppose that even the world itself could not contain the books that should be written" (21:25). Even taking into account the hyperbole, this still acclaims the illumination of the Holy Spirit in shedding abroad the light of God upon the memories of Jesus' apostles—and others.

Still there were so many things that Jesus wanted to teach his followers which they were not yet ready to hear. Furthermore, much which they had heard they did not fully understand. After the resurrection Jesus spent much time prior to his ascension interpreting to them the Old Testament in the light of what had happened (Luke 24:44–48). Even just before the ascension their minds were cluttered and clouded with confusion as to the nature of the kingdom of God (Acts 1:6–7). Among other things, this was one reason why they were to wait in Jerusalem before launching forth to preach the gospel of the kingdom (Luke 24:49; Acts 1:8). They were to wait for the coming of the Holy Spirit.

How clear and certain was the sound of the gospel trumpet at Pentecost and beyond! Why? Because their minds were now illumined by the Holy Spirit. The prophecies of the Old Testament and the teachings and the redemptive act of Jesus came into focus. This explains the clear record of the Gospels, the preaching in Acts, the Christology of the Epistles, and the prophecies of Revelation.

Remembrance of truth and guidance into truth! It is impossible to explain the New Testament apart from the illumination of the Holy Spirit.

Inspired

Inspiration is the divine act whereby the messenger who delivers or records the message is guided and controlled in his work (cf. 2 Tim. 3:16). The English word comes from the Latin verb which means *to breathe in*. This does not mean that the person involved made no effort to ascertain the facts involved in the revelation (cf. Luke 1:1–4). Inspiration involves not only the divine activity but the whole of the human personality.

There are many theories as to the nature of inspiration. The naturalistic theory says that God is in all men, therefore all men are inspired. The degrees of inspiration depend upon one's mental and spiritual capacity. Obviously this is not the biblical idea of inspiration. Another theory is that inspiration actually is illumination rather than infallible guidance into truth. This theory holds to varying degrees of truth and of error in the Bible.

The claim of inerrancy for the Bible, of course, relates to the original manuscripts, none of which is available for examination. Every serious student of the Scriptures knows that rather insignificant additions appear in later copies of various manuscripts.

But these are due to copyists, not to the original writers. There is no divine inspiration to protect copyists any more than there is for modern typesetters. But fortunately as older manuscripts have been discovered and studied these additions have been largely eliminated.

The so-called discrepancies in the Bible are due to a lack of knowledge and understanding on the part of the interpreter. Many of these have been cleared up by additional knowledge derived from archaeological discoveries and research. In such instances the Bible has been vindicated.

More to the point are two other theories of inspiration. The plenary verbal theory says that every word of the Scriptures was divinely selected and dictated to the writers, who themselves were only stenographers. One form of this theory is called dynamical inspiration, where the thought, not the language, was inspired. The writers were thus enabled to declare truth without error, but were permitted to transmit this truth in words of their own selection. As one notes the imprint of each writer's personality upon his work, it appears that this last theory comes nearest to the truth.

But, as Mullins points out, no one theory can exhaust the divine operation in inspiration.

The true method, on the contrary, is to study the Bible inductively in order to learn what its claims are and what success it has had in meeting those claims, in the experience of Christians of the past and present. This is the experiential and practical method of approaching the doctrine of inspiration. It is much more concerned with the result than it is with the process of inspiration.[3]

It is difficult for us to make a sharp distinction at all times between revelation, illumination, and inspiration. They are intermingled in the process. But one thing is clear—the entire process is the work of the Holy Spirit. He is God's Spirit sent forth to reveal God to man, and through Jesus Christ, to illuminate men's minds to understand the revelation, and to guide chosen men to record the revelation "without any mixture of error." It is to this work of the Holy Spirit that we now turn.

As the Holy Spirit gave the revelation of God and illumined men to comprehend it, he also inspired chosen men to proclaim and record it. The Bible makes this claim for itself.

In 2 Peter, the apostle is discussing the person and work of Jesus as God in the flesh. He insists that he is not following "cunningly devised fables" (1:16) but is speaking from personal experience. Then he refers to the transfiguration (cf. Matt. 17), claiming that that event confirmed the Old Testament prophecies concerning the Messiah.

In 1:20, he says "that no prophecy of the scripture is of any private interpretation." More accurately, "No prophecy of Scripture comes out of private disclosure." [4] This refers to the prophets' grasp of truth, not the reader's interpretation of it. That this is the sense is seen in the following verse. Literally, "For not by the will of man was prophecy borne along at any time; but by being borne along from time to time of the Holy Spirit men spoke from God."

Note the verbs "borne along" (*pherō*). The former is an aorist passive tense of point action. The latter is a present passive participle of repeated action or action occurring from time to time as the case demanded it.

So prophecy is of divine origin, not human. "No prophet starts a prophecy himself. He is not a self-starter." [5] R. H. Strachan is quite helpful at this point.

Here we have the only reference to the Holy Spirit in the Epistle, and only in this connexion, vis. as the source of prophetic inspiration. The spirit is an agency rather than an agent. The men speak. The spirit impels. It is of much significance for the interpretation of the whole passage that *anthrōpoi* [men] occupies a position of emphasis at the end of the sentence [Greek text], thus bringing into prominence the human agent.[6]

Peter makes it clear that the human agent is not self-inspired. He is inspired by the Holy Spirit.

Second Timothy 3:16 expresses the source or means of inspiration: "All scripture is given by inspiration of God." Literally, "All scripture is God-breathed" (*Theopneustos*). Even those who are not versed in the Greek language can see this picture. *Theos* is God. *Pneustos* is a form of the verb *pneō* from which comes the word *pneuma,* meaning breath, wind, or spirit.

The word *Theopneustos* is a rare word found only here in the New Testament. A form of this word is found in the papyri with the sense of divine inspiration. As Paul uses it, it means that all Scripture is the result of God's breathing into the human agent who records it. This is the meaning of inspiration. For the purpose of recording the Scriptures, God sent forth his Spirit into his chosen vessels to guide them in the process. This is implied in repeated references throughout the Bible.

"Moses wrote all the words of the Lord" (Ex. 24:4; Deut. 31:9). The prophets were commanded to write down their visions and messages (Isa. 30:8; Jer. 30:2; 36:1–2,28; Ezek. 43:11). Jesus' promise of the Holy Spirit's guidance included the inspiration of the Scriptures. Paul repeatedly states that he preached and wrote by divine guidance (Rom. 1:1–7; 1 Cor. 11:23 ff.; Gal. 1:11–12). John wrote Revelation under the guidance of the Spirit (1:10).

In inspiration the Holy Spirit worked directly in and through the writer. But this did not rule out the personality and cooperation of the agent. For instance, it is largely an accepted fact of New Testament study that Matthew and Luke built their gospels about the framework of Mark, at the same time drawing upon other sources of material. John evidently was familiar with the other three Gospels as through his own, among other purposes, he sought to supplement their works.

The clearest example of the divine-human element in inspiration is found in Luke 1:1–4, ASV:

Forasmuch as many have taken in hand to draw up a narrative concerning those matters which have been fulfilled among us, even as they delivered them unto us, who from the beginning were eyewitnesses and ministers of the word, it seemed good to me also, having traced the course of all things accurately from the first, to write unto thee in [chronological] order, most excellent Theophilus; that thou mightest know the certainty concerning the things wherein thou wast instructed.

Several things stand out in this statement. First, Luke had a purpose in writing (v.4). Second, he had access to earlier written records (v.1). Third, he interviewed eyewitnesses of the events (v.2). Fourth, he evaluated his information, tracing all things accurately from beginning to end of the story (v.3). Fifth, he wrote his Gospel in chronological order (v.3).

Luke was especially equipped for this sort of thing. He was a physician-scientist. He had the sense of a historian. He spent two years in Palestine during Paul's Caesarean imprisonment. During this time he had ample opportunity to gather and study written records and to interview and record the accounts of those who had been with Jesus. It is possible that among those may have been Mary herself. He knew how to ferret out facts, sift out chaff, and evaluate evidence. And he wrote with consummate skill. The result is the most beautiful account of the life of Jesus on record. The accepted accuracy of his Gospel has served to strengthen the case for the historical accuracy of the other Gospels.

But we are not to suppose that a writer who places such emphasis upon the Holy Spirit was a "self-starter" or regarded himself as such. His Gospel was not borne along by the will of man. It was borne along by the Holy Spirit as Luke wrote for God. He was "God-breathed," as through inspiration he was guided by the Holy Spirit in his purpose, research, evaluation, and recording of the Gospel which bears his name.

Only by the inspiration of the Holy Spirit could this Greek physician record the most beautiful story of the virgin birth of Jesus. And the most complete account of the bodily resurrection from the dead.

Yea, we can say more. Only by the inspiration of the Holy Spirit can we explain how these wonderful books, written by approximately fifty-seven different authors from almost as many different walks of life, and over a span of fifteen hundred years in places ranging from Babylon to Rome, when gathered into one volume, comprise a whole.

If someone unaware of the Old Testament should read the New Testament, he would ask, "Where is that which came before?" Should he, unaware of the New Testament, read the Old, he would ask, "Where is the rest of the story?"

The Holy Spirit—revealing, illuminating, inspiring. The result —the Book above all books—God's Holy Bible. He is the same Holy Spirit who in this hour illumines the minds of those who prayerfully read its pages that men may drink from its inexhaustible fountain of Truth and feed upon its living Bread.

Postascension Work

It is the purpose of this chapter to examine the teachings of Jesus concerning the postascension work of the Holy Spirit as they appear in John 14–16. They were given in the intimacy of the little band of apostles (except Judas) who had been with Jesus for the greater part of his public ministry.

After the apostles had grasped the truth that their Lord was to be crucified, they were in a state of sorrowful shock. Seeing this, Jesus spoke to them the words which have formed a pillow of faith for bereaved, troubled hearts through the ages (14:1–6).

Following a period of questions and answers, he sought to prepare them for the future, a future in which they would be without his bodily presence. And his words centered in the place which the Holy Spirit would occupy in their lives and ministry after he, Jesus, had returned to the Father.

As the "Other Jesus"

Jesus began by assuring them that after his departure they would not be alone: "I will pray the Father, and he shall give you another Comforter" (14:16). Thus he spoke of the Holy Spirit (cf. v.26).

The heart of this promise is the word "another." It renders a Greek word meaning "another of the same kind." So the Lord

said that the Father would send *another of the same kind* as Jesus
to be with his people. Commenting on this word, B. H. Carroll,
in his book *The Holy Spirit,* called the Holy Spirit "the other
Jesus." Marcus Dods has called him Jesus' *alter ego* or Jesus'
other self.[1]

The Holy Spirit's spiritual presence will take the place of Jesus'
bodily presence. God would still be with them, but his presence
would be manifest in his Spirit rather than in the earthly sojourn
of his Son.

As such, the Holy Spirit will be their "comforter." Actually this
word is more of a derived meaning growing out of the Greek
word so translated.

In Job 16:2, (Septuagint, Greek translation of the Old Testament) a kindred word is translated "comforters" (KJV). This
word in John 14:16 has been transliterated into English as
Paraclete. It comes from a compound verb composed of *para,*
alongside (note our word "parallel"), and *kaleō,* I call. So the
Paraclete is the *one being called alongside.* In the New Testament
this word appears only five times and always in the writings of
John. Four times it is found in the Gospel (14:16,26; 15:26;
16:7). It is also used in 1 John 2:1, where it is translated
"advocate." Here it is rendered by the Latin *ad voco,* to call to,
which is the equivalent of the Greek verb.

Now what did the word "paraclete" mean? It was used to refer
to a lawyer in a court of justice, especially the one for defense. A
man must appear in court. So he procures a lawyer to be called
alongside him to plead his case. In this sense he will be a pleader
or an advocate.

Mullins, after suggesting several translations of this word as
advocate, intercessor, or helper, concludes that perhaps the best
one is simply Paraclete. To one versed in the Greek language
perhaps this is true. But, otherwise, in the broadest sense, perhaps

the best purely English translation would be "helper." The Holy
Spirit is the one being called alongside us as our helper, whether
it be in intercession or in some other time of need.

The fact that the Holy Spirit was to be another of the same
kind of Paraclete, means that Jesus also was a Paraclete. This
we find to be true, as stated in 1 John 2:1: "If any man sin [any
Christian], we have an advocate [paraclete] with the Father."
Literally, "face to face with" or "before the Father." He is before
the Father to plead for the forgiveness of a repentant Christian
who has sinned.

While the word is not used, there are many times when Jesus
was the advocate for the disciples. For instance, in John 17 he
prayed for them (vv.9 ff.). Knowing that they faced severe trials,
he prayed that the Father would keep or guard them. Since they
would remain in the world to do his work, he prayed that the
Father would protect them from the evil one who would assail
them. Furthermore, in Gethsemane, upon being arrested Jesus
pleaded that the disciples might not be taken also. This within
itself was an advocacy before men, even as he is the advocate
before the Father. Likewise, throughout their sojourn with Jesus
he had been their helper, guide, teacher, encourager, comforter,
and strength. He had stood alongside them as together they had
done the work of the Father. He had truly been their helper.

Now Jesus is to be taken from them. So he promises that the
Father will give them another advocate or helper of the same
kind as he had been. He would be their advocate in their trials
before men. Already we have noted Jesus' promise that the Holy
Spirit would plead their cases when they were brought before
both religious and political tribunals. Now this is to become a
reality. Furthermore, he will be their advocate before God. He
will, when necessary, assist them in their praying.

At times one's longings are too deep for words. It is then that
"the Spirit also helpeth our infirmities: for we know not what

we should pray for as we ought: but the Spirit itself maketh intercession for us with groanings which cannot be uttered [sighs
that baffle words]. And he that searcheth the hearts knoweth
what is the mind of the Spirit, because he maketh intercession
for the saints according to the will of God" (Rom. 8:26–27).

This rather mysterious passage is most beautiful in the Greek
text. It pictures a man who comes upon another who has a heavy
burden which he cannot lift, so he comes to his aid. He gets on one
side of the burden across from and face to face with the troubled
man who is trying without success to lift his load. Then, putting
his hands underneath his side of the other man's burden, he
helps him to lift it—together they lift the load.

In like fashion the Holy Spirit helps us to pray. Sometimes we
have a prayer so heavy with concern that we are unable to put
it into words or to lift it up before God. Finding us in this condition, the Holy Spirit lends a hand. He helps our weakness. Through
our concern and faith and the Spirit's power our prayer is lifted
before the throne of grace. For God knows the mind of the
Spirit who interprets our prayers to him. Thus the Holy Spirit is
our helper, truly a helper in time of need (cf. Heb. 4:16).

But this help goes beyond the crisis moments in our lives. The
Holy Spirit is our helper as he instructs, guides, empowers, encourages, consoles, and does innumerable things for and in us as
we seek to serve the Lord.

This *help,* of course, assumes that we are in the will of God,
which means that we are available to him for his work. Men often
pray for the Holy Spirit to come upon them. But notice that Jesus
said, "I will pray the Father, and he shall give you another Paraclete." The Holy Spirit was sent forth of God to do his work,
and in answer to Jesus' prayer, not ours. Our prayer should be that
we may confess our sins, receive God's forgiveness, and make ourselves available to the Spirit's power as our helper.

Furthermore, as "the other Jesus" the Holy Spirit is an abiding presence. The promise is "that he may abide [make his home] with you for ever" (John 14:16). What a glorious promise! The apostles thought that they were to be alone in a hostile world. But now they are promised the presence of God in the Holy Spirit, a presence which will not be taken away. He would enable them to do even greater works than Jesus had done in his brief earthly ministry (v.12). Not greater in degree but in scope. For this to happen Jesus must go to the Father, that the Father may send the Spirit (16:7).

When he comes, he will be to the disciples all that Jesus had been to them in fellowship and service. Yea, he would be more—in degree. Jesus had walked alongside the disciples; the Holy Spirit will dwell in them. Jesus had spoken to them in audible tones; the Spirit will speak within their spirits. Jesus worked with them; the Spirit will work in them. At times they were away from Jesus' bodily presence. Never will they be away from the Holy Spirit. Jesus was with them on earth for only a few years. But the Spirit will be with them forever. Jesus' promise to be with them "always, even unto the end of the world" was the promise of his presence through "the other Jesus" (Matt. 28:20).

This suggests our Lord's further promise. "I will not leave you comfortless [orphanous, orphans]: I will come to you" (John 14:18). This could, and in part most likely does, refer to his appearances after the resurrection. "Yet a little while, and the world seeth me no more; but ye see me: because I live, ye shall live also. At that day ye shall know that I am in my Father, and ye in me, and I in you" (vv.19–20). The world did not see him after his dead body was placed in the tomb, for there is no record that anyone other than believers saw him after the resurrection. But the faithful saw him, and in doing so fully knew that the Father was in him. However, even this does not fully satisfy Jesus' words. The disciples were to know him in that continuing fellowship as they were "in Christ" and he was in them. Indeed, they were not left as orphans.

And this realization was made possible through the coming of "the other Jesus." This is one of those elements in which Jesus and the Spirit are distinct and yet are identical in their work. The Holy Spirit did not replace Jesus. His ministry made Jesus more real.

Mullins raises and answers a most vital question in this regard.

Is the Paraclete, then, the successor or the substitute for Christ as He is sometimes called? The answer is that He is both and neither. He is the successor of Christ historically, but not in the sense that Christ ceases to act in the church. He is the substitute for Christ's physical presence, but only in order that He may make vital and actual Christ's spiritual presence. As we have seen, the Paraclete moves only in the range of truths conveyed in and through Christ as the historical manifestation of God. A "Kingdom of the Spirit," therefore, is impossible in the Christian sense, save as the historical Jesus is made the basis of the Spirit's action in history.[2]

As Teacher

Jesus called the Holy Spirit "the Spirit of truth" (14:17; cf. v.6). He is qualified by, gives, and defends truth against the evil spirit of error (cf. 1 John 4:1–7). And this suggests his role as teacher.

The role of teacher was a major one in Jesus' ministry. Yet he could teach his disciples only to the extent that they could receive and comprehend it. Even much that he taught them fell upon dull minds until they were illuminated by the Holy Spirit.

Jesus said, "These things have I spoken unto you, being yet present with you" (John 14:25); literally, "alongside you abiding." Later in the evening he added, "I have yet many things to say unto you, but ye cannot bear them now" (16:12). Even the greatest Teacher who ever lived was limited, not by his knowledge, but by the ability of his pupils to understand. This is the very nature of progressive revelation. However, the teaching of Jesus did not end with his bodily departure from the earth. What he had begun "the other Jesus" would complete.

"But the Comforter [Paraclete, helper], which is the Holy Ghost [Spirit] (note that here Jesus clearly identifies the Paraclete as the Holy Spirit), whom the Father will send in my name, he shall teach you all things, and bring all things to your remembrance, whatsoever I have said unto you" (14:26).

Already we have touched upon this verse, especially with regard to the illumination of the memories of the apostles. Beyond that, the Holy Spirit would teach them all things. "All things" does not refer to the sum total of all knowledge, scientific and otherwise. This means a full understanding of Christ and his redemptive work, as well as the knowledge necessary for living the Christian life and for prosecuting God's redemptive mission to all men.

Now this teaching by the Holy Spirit involved at least two things. First, it involved his interpretation of the things that Jesus had taught. Two things will suffice to illustrate this point.

One has to do with the universal nature of the gospel. The disciples were so filled with current Jewish prejudice against all non-Jews that they had extreme difficulty in grasping this. To them salvation and the kingdom of God were for Jews only. A current rabbinical idea was that Gentiles were but fuel for hell. Jesus' experience with the Syrophoenician woman was largely an acted parable to demonstrate to his disciples how vicious was this attitude (cf. Matt. 15:21 ff.). But even just before his ascension his little band still was clinging to the Jewish idea of the kingdom (Acts 1:16). It took a vision at Joppa and a demonstration of the Holy Spirit at Caesarea to straighten out Peter's thinking in this regard (Acts 10). Later he made the astounding statement (i.e., for a Jew), "But we believe that through the grace of the Lord Jesus Christ *we* [Jews] shall be saved, even as *they* [Gentiles]" (author's italics, Acts 15:11).

This was a complete reversal of thought. The Jews had been saying that Gentiles must be saved by first becoming Jewish proselytes. Now Peter says that Jews and Gentiles are saved as *such,* and *alike,* both through the grace of the Lord Jesus Christ. Romans 1–11 is an extended statement of the same idea. Only through the teaching of the Holy Spirit could either Peter or Paul have grasped the meaning of Jesus' teachings in this regard.

Another such teaching had to do with the meaning of the death and resurrection of Jesus. The idea of a crucified Saviour was unthinkable to Jesus' contemporaries. To the Jews it was a stumbling block, and to the Greeks it was foolishness (cf. 1 Cor. 1:23). When at Caesarea-Philippi, Jesus taught *clearly,* in plain words, about his death and resurrection, Peter "began to rebuke him, saying, Be it far from thee, Lord: this shall not be unto thee" (Matt. 16:22). The fact that he "began" suggests that he continued to seek to dissuade Jesus from such a course.

Yet on the day of Pentecost this same Peter preached, "Him, being delivered by the determinate counsel and foreknowledge of God, ye have taken, and by wicked hands have crucified and slain: whom God hath raised up, . . . therefore being by the right hand of God exalted, and having received of the Father the promise of the Holy Ghost [Spirit], he hath shed forth this, which ye now see and hear. . . . Therefore let all the house of Israel know assuredly, that God hath made that same Jesus, whom ye have crucified, both Lord and Christ" (Acts 2:23–36; cf. 3:15; 4:10–12).

What effected this change in Peter? Jesus' death and resurrection, and his postresurrection teaching (cf. Luke 24:44 ff.)? Yes.

But as Acts 1:6 shows, it was still not clear to the apostles. The full answer centers in the teaching of the Holy Spirit as he illuminated the minds of the apostles.

It certainly did not come through human reason, as Paul clearly shows in 1 Corinthians. This "stumbling block" and "foolishness" he declares to be "Christ the power of God, and the wisdom of God" (1:24). That which the Jews considered weakness and the Greeks regarded as moronic was to God power and wisdom. How did Paul discern this true meaning of the crucifixion? Through the teachings of the Holy Spirit. For "God hath revealed them unto us by his Spirit: for the Spirit searcheth all things, yea, the deep things of God. . . . the things of God knoweth no man, but the Spirit of God. . . . Which things also we speak, not in the words which man's wisdom teacheth, but which the Holy Ghost [Spirit] teacheth; comparing spiritual things with spiritual" (2:10–13).

Second, the Spirit's teaching involved revelations. Paul is a prime example of this, as was John in Revelation. Since we have already discussed these matters we shall pass them by with a brief comment. While these were true revelations, they were based in measure upon things which Jesus had taught and done. But they involved those further things which Jesus did not teach specifically, since the disciples were not yet ready to receive them. The great body of Pauline Christology, as well as that of the epistle to the Hebrews, is one example. The "mystery of Christ" concerning the Jews and Gentiles being gathered into one body through Christ is another (cf. Eph. 3). And certainly some elements of revelation come in the category of "things to come" (John 16:13).

How meager would be our understanding of the great things of Christ without the Holy Spirit as teacher. For even our understanding of the Bible as a whole comes as he guides us into all truth (cf. John 16:13). Not just any exposition of the Scriptures is truth necessarily, despite the wisdom of the expositor. We must not discount the value of knowledge. But knowledge alone is no substitute for the teaching of the Holy Spirit. The Holy Spirit does not contradict himself. When the Christian surrenders his mind and its knowledge, be it great or little, to the guidance of the Holy Spirit, he will guide into truth—truth that corresponds to all truth as revealed in Jesus Christ. For he who has the mind of the Spirit has "the mind of Christ" (1 Cor. 2:16).

Bearing Witness

Jesus speaks of the Holy Spirit as one who will bear witness concerning him. "When the Comforter [Helper] is come, whom I will send unto you from the Father, even the Spirit of truth, which proceedeth from the Father, he shall testify of me" (John 15:26).

In passing, it is of interest to note that Jesus says that he will send the Spirit. In John 14:16, he said that the Father would send him in answer to his prayer. But in John 15:26, Jesus says, "I will send." The personal pronoun "I" is written out in the Greek text, which makes it emphatic. But he will send the Holy Spirit "from [*para,* alongside] the Father," and he "proceedeth from [*para,* from alongside] the Father." There is no contradiction here. It is another of those examples of the intimate relation of the Father and Son in God's work.

The emphasis, of course, is upon the Holy Spirit as witness. "He shall testify [*martureō,* bear witness] of [*peri,* concerning, about] me." In the papyri the basic idea in *martureō* is that of giving legal testimony of what one has seen or experienced.[3] It was a common practice to write this word after a signature in the sense that we write the word "witness." For example, a will is so witnessed. "I, Serapion, am witness."

John 21:24 gives a striking example of the use of this verb and its noun form. Literally, "This is the disciple, the one giving eyewitness testimony of these things, and the one who wrote these things: and we [note the plural] know that his evidence is true." Some group, probably the Ephesian elders, appended this statement to the Fourth Gospel, attesting the author and his material. In essence this verse means, "We, the Ephesian elders, are witnesses."

So, in effect, Jesus said that the Holy Spirit would write, "I am witness" to our Lord's life and work (cf. 1 John 5:7-10). Not only does the Spirit authenticate the record of Jesus, but he also gives eyewitness testimony in the hearts of men (cf. John 16:8-14). This fact is evident not only in the Scriptures, it is seen in practical experience through the ages, even today.

Furthermore, Jesus says, "Ye also shall bear witness, because ye have been with me from the beginning" (John 15:27). "Ye" (emphatic) in contradistinction to the Holy Spirit. Or, better still, the apostles are to add their testimony to that of the Holy Spirit. He will witness through them, but their testimony will not be hearsay evidence, even from the Holy Spirit, for they have been with Jesus from the beginning, or throughout his public ministry. They have seen the Holy Spirit work in and through Jesus. His teaching, mighty works, yea, his death and resurrection, and his saving power—all will be firsthand testimony from them.

In a sense this is true of every Christian witness. Only those who were with Jesus in the flesh can give firsthand testimony to that fact. But every believer in faith can bear evidence of his experience which is rooted in the historical fact of the incarnation. On this basis he can write, "I am witness" to the saving and ministering work of Jesus. But, as with the apostles so with us, this witness is made both personal and powerful as the Holy Spirit witnesses to us and through us.

Glorifying Christ

This work of the Holy Spirit is actually the outgrowth or purpose of his work as teacher and witness. For Jesus climaxed all of his teaching concerning his relationship to the Holy Spirit by saying, "He shall glorify me" (John 16:14). Here again "he" (*ekeinos*) is written out, and so is emphatic.

Thus we may speak of the altruism of the Holy Spirit. He does not glorify himself, but Jesus. Now two significant things evolve from this truth. In the first place, this explains why it is so difficult for us to comprehend the Holy Spirit. So often someone says, "I can understand Jesus, but I cannot understand the Holy Spirit." This, in part, describes the common experience of all Christians. And it is as it should be, for the Holy Spirit does not speak of or interpret himself. He unveils to us the person and work of Jesus. He never points to himself, but to Jesus. Your growing comprehension of Jesus is the work of the Holy Spirit in you.

In the second place, this suggests that any religion or system of theology which magnifies the Holy Spirit above Jesus is not of the Holy Spirit! It is the work of another spirit. Every so-called spiritual demonstration is not necessarily a work of the Holy Spirit. For 1 John 4:1 says, "Beloved, believe not every spirit, but try [judge between] the spirits whether they are of God: because many false prophets are gone out into the world."

John contrasts the "spirit of truth, and the spirit of error" (v.6). In other words, there is an *evil* spirit—the spirit of the evil one— at work in the world. Certainly this evil spirit will do all that he can to detract from Jesus. He will even enable men to do signs and wonders by which to "deceive the very elect" (Matt. 24:24). Even the ecstatic gifts of the Holy Spirit, as seen in the New Testament, are temporary in nature. Contrary to much popular opinion the book of Acts places very little emphasis upon these. And Paul places all of these in a secondary place (see chap. 9).

The ministry of the Holy Spirit is to magnify Jesus. "He shall glorify me," said Jesus. And even though the power and work of the Holy Spirit are of great importance, he stands in the background that in all things Jesus Christ may have the preeminence.

Robertson says, "This is the glory of the Holy Spirit, to glorify Jesus Christ." [4]

This truth is clearly demonstrated in the manner in which the Holy Spirit does his work: "He shall receive [take] of mine, and shall shew it unto you" (John 16:14). Literally, "Out of the things of mine he shall take, and shall declare to you." The Spirit's teaching shall be about Jesus, not about himself. This is a reavowal of what Jesus had said in the preceding verse. The Holy Spirit "shall not speak of [apo, from] himself; but whatsoever he shall hear, that shall he speak" (v.13). What the Father tells him, he will speak. The complete revelation of the Father is in the Son. So of this alone will the Spirit speak.

Marcus Dods says, "The Spirit draws from no other source of information or inspiration. It is always 'out of that which is Christ's' He furnishes the Church. So only could he glorify Christ. Not by taking the Church beyond Christ, but by more fully exhibiting the fulness of Christ, does He fulfil His mission." [5]

No statement or system of thought which degrades Jesus is of the Holy Spirit. Neither can one exalt him apart from the work of the Holy Spirit. First Corinthians 12:3 says, "No man speaking by the Spirit of God calleth Jesus accursed [anathema Iēsous, Jesus is anathema, a curse concerning him]: and that no man can say that Jesus is the Lord [Kurios Iēsous, Lord Jesus or Jesus is Lord], but by the Holy Ghost [Spirit]." Anathema Jesus was most likely blasphemous language used by the Jews (cf. Acts 13:45; 18:6). Such, says Paul, is not of the Holy Spirit. In emperor worship the Romans sought to require everyone to say, "Caesar is lord." To refuse was to be in danger of death for treason. Christians refused, saying instead, "Jesus is Lord" (cf. Rom. 10:9). Paul says that such could be said only through the Holy Spirit.

Another prime example of the Spirit's work in glorifying Jesus in the face of hostile forces was related to gnosticism. This philosophy regarded God as absolutely good and matter as absolutely evil. To explain the creation of matter they posited a series of beings emanating from God in descending order. Each being, called an *aeon,* possessed deity, but each had less than the preceding one. The lowest *aeon* had enough deity to create, but so little as to be able to create evil matter. When they came into contact with Christianity, they made Christ the lowest *aeon* who created the universe. But this reduced Christ from full deity to the role of a demigod, almost a demon.

What was the Holy Spirit's answer to this system of thought? It is seen primarily in the Gospel of John, 1 John, and Colossians. In the prologue to John's Gospel (1:1–18), Christ is declared as the fulness of deity, the creator of every single part of the universe, the source of all life, and the one coming in flesh as Jesus Christ to reveal in redemption God's fulness of grace and truth. Literally, "In the beginning always was the Word [Christ], and the Word always was equal with God, and the Word always was God himself. . . . Every single part of the universe came into being through him; and apart from him came into being not even one thing which has come into being. In him always was life; . . . And the Word became flesh, and dwelt among us . . . full of grace and truth" (1:1–14). This tremendous statement came through the Holy Spirit.

First John 4:2–3 says, "Hereby know ye the Spirit of God: Every spirit that confesseth that Jesus Christ is come in the flesh is of God: And every spirit that confesseth not that Jesus Christ is come in the flesh is not of God."

Through Paul, in Colossians, the Holy Spirit declares the same great truth. Literally, "Who is the express image of the invisible God, the Lord of all creation: For *in the sphere* of him and him alone was created the universe as a whole . . . the universe as a whole *through* him and *unto* him stands created . . . and he is before every single part of the universe, and the universe as a whole in him *holds together*. And he is the head of the body, the church" (1:15–18, author's italics). Thus Jesus Christ is declared to be the source, intermediate agent, and the goal of all creation. He is the center of the universe, the head of the church—the redeemed of all the ages.

There is no greater statement of the deity of Jesus Christ than that found in Colossians 2:9. Literally, "Because in him and him alone is continuously abiding all the very essence of deity, the state of being God in bodily form." In this one verse Paul exhausted the power of language to answer the Gnostics and to exalt Jesus Christ. He wrote under the inspiration of the Holy Spirit. Only as he was "God-breathed" could he have made so stupendous a statement.

Through the apostle Paul, the Holy Spirit erected this pinnacle of truth as a landmark to all who love the Lord Jesus Christ sincerely. It is a bulwark against all of the onslaughts of the "spirit of error" who would diminish one whit the superlative glory of him who is the crowning revelation of the redeeming love of God.

Truly, "He shall glorify me: for he shall receive of mine, and shall shew it unto you" (John 16:14).

Work of Redemption

7

Evangelism is one of the truly great words in the Christian vocabulary. Yet it is not distinctly a Christian word. "To evangelize" is simply a transliteration of the Greek verb meaning to bring good news. It is so used in the Septuagint. The Greek papyri uses it of one announcing a military victory. The title *evangelist* is found on a pagan inscription to refer to the person who announced the oracles of the Greek shrine at Daphne.

In the strictly New Testament sense this family of words, including "evangel" or "gospel" (from the Anglo-Saxon "god spel," glad tidings), has reference to declaring the good news of the kingdom of God, the salvation provided in Christ, and matters pertaining to this salvation.

This evangelism is made possible through the redemptive work of God in Christ. But through the ages it is proclaimed and made effective through the work of the Holy Spirit.

On the night before his death, Jesus taught his apostles about their obligation in the redemptive purpose of God. He reminded them that they had been chosen and appointed to go forth and produce fruit in the kingdom (John 15:16). This fruit will be souls won to Christ and developed in their kingdom relationship. Because they believe in him, the apostles will do the work of evangelism that he has done (14:12). In scope their work will

91

even exceed his (v.12). This promise is extended to all of the followers of Jesus through the ages.

And why is this possible? "Because I go unto my Father" (v.12). This would be a strange promise, indeed, except for that which follows. For it is in Jesus' going to the Father that the Father will send the Holy Spirit (vv.16–17). The Holy Spirit, therefore, will continue the evangelism which Jesus had initiated. He will do so as he empowers and guides the followers of Jesus. He will do so as he enlivens the written word of God to do its work (Heb. 4:12 ff.; Eph. 6:17). And he will do so as he works in the hearts of lost men and in the lives of the saints. It is to these last two that we shall address ourselves in this chapter.

At this point, therefore, it is well to note the scope of evangelism in the larger sense. Too often we think of evangelism only in the sense of regeneration. The result is that we produce a multitude of spiritual pygmies. Someone asked Gaines S. Dobbins if conversion were not the end of salvation. He replied, "Yes, but which end?" The scope of evangelism involves regeneration, sanctification, and glorification.

A. Regeneration, or the new birth, is a work of God's grace whereby believers become new creatures in Christ Jesus. It is a change of heart wrought by the Holy Spirit through conviction of sin, to which the sinner responds in repentance toward God and faith in the Lord Jesus Christ.

Repentance and faith are inseparable experiences of grace. Repentance is a genuine turning from sin toward God. Faith is the acceptance of Jesus Christ and commitment of the entire personality to Him as Lord and Saviour. Justification is God's gracious and full acquittal upon principles of His righteousness of all sinners who repent and believe in Christ. Justification brings the believer into a relationship of peace and favor with God.

B. Sanctification is the experience, beginning in regeneration, by which the believer is set apart to God's purposes, and is enabled to progress toward moral and spiritual perfection through the presence and power of the Holy Spirit dwelling in him. Growth in grace should continue throughout the regenerate person's life.

C. Glorification is the culmination of salvation and is the final blessed and abiding state of the redeemed.[1]

Regeneration

Regeneration is the Holy Spirit's work with lost men. Second Corinthians 5:17 says that "if any man be in Christ, he is a new creature [creation]: old things are passed away; behold, all things are become new." While the provision for this new creation is in Christ, it is effected through the work of the Holy Spirit. The Holy Spirit works with the lost sinner that he may become a new creation in Christ. And this he does through conviction, repentance, faith, and the new birth.

Jesus said that when the Spirit "is come, he will reprove [convince, convict] the world of sin, and of righteousness, and of judgment: Of sin, because they believe not on me; of righteousness, because I go to my Father, and ye see me no more; of judgment, because the prince of this world is judged" (John 16:8–11). In this sense the Holy Spirit is Christ's advocate with the world. He is also the world's helper in enabling lost men to come to Christ.

In the Greek text, the emphasis is on the Holy Spirit. Literally, "Coming, that one [ekeinos] will convict the world concerning sin . . . righteousness . . . judgment." Conviction, then, is the work of the Holy Spirit. The verb rendered "convince" or "convict" means to press home a conviction. The spirit, therefore, presses home to sinful hearts the threefold truth concerning sin, righteousness, and judgment.

Of sin, because they believe not on me.—As the Spirit presses home the truth about sin, the lost man sees it for the heinous thing that it is. Not an animal instinct or glandular disturbance which carries no moral responsibility, but as rebellion against God—a missing of the mark of God's will and character (cf. Rom. 3:23). Through the Holy Spirit he sees at Calvary not merely what sin does to him but what it did/does to God. Furthermore, he realizes that the greatest sin is failure to believe in Jesus Christ as his Saviour, a rejection of all that God in Christ has done to reconcile him to God (John 3:18; 2 Cor. 5:19).

Of righteousness, because I go to the Father, and ye see me no more.—This is the opposite of sin. From convicting of sin the Holy Spirit points to the righteousness of God in Christ Jesus (cf. Rom. 10:4 ff.). The sinner is made to see how far short of this righteousness he falls, and how impossible it is for him to achieve it in his own power (cf. Rom. 10:3). He knows that it can come only through an act of God, which he can receive only through faith (cf. Rom. 1:16–17).

Jesus' exaltation by the Father will be the proof of his righteousness as that which is demanded of God. This within itself will be used of the Spirit to cause men to desire more than a worldly standard of righteousness.

Of judgment, because the prince of this world is [has been] judged.—The cross and resurrection handed down a full and final condemnatory judgment against Satan. God's complete triumph over him and his evil designs proved the judgment that had always been in God's heart against all manner of evil. But in this historical demonstration God left no doubt about it. And as Marcus Dods says, "The distinction between sin and righteousness was, under the Spirit's teaching, to become absolute. In the crucifixion of Christ the influences which moved worldly men . . . were finally condemned. . . . The world, the prince of it, is 'judged.' To adhere to it rather than to Christ is to cling to a doomed cause, a sinking ship." [2]

Thus the lost man convicted of judgment is faced with a choice: Either he must cling to Satan and knowingly accept hell, or else he must receive Christ and accept his wonderful salvation and the glory of heaven.

But the Holy Spirit is not through with him. For he continues to work, endeavoring to lead him to a true repentance.

There are two Greek words translated "repent" in the New Testament. One means a worldly sorrow or regret that one's actions did not produce the desired result, or that one is faced with direful consequences because of his deeds. But it involves no change of nature. For instance, this word is used in Matthew 27:3 to describe Judas' *repentance*. He merely regretted his action because of its consequences. This verb is used only six times in the New Testament (Matt. 21:29,32; 27:3; 2 Cor. 7:8; Heb. 7:21).

The other word for "repent" means a change of heart, mind, and attitude. It involves a change of nature. The verb form is used in the New Testament thirty-four times. The noun "repentance" is found twenty-four times.

A contrast between these two verbs for "repent" may be seen in the two thieves on the cross. The rebellious one merely regretted that his crimes had brought him to the cross; he had no change of heart. Had he escaped, he would most likely have returned to a life of crime. Had he not, it would simply have been out of fear of the consequences. He was still a criminal at heart. But the other thief experienced true repentance. He did not ask to be delivered from the cross but to be saved from sin. His was a new attitude, heart, and mind.

One of the clearest contrasts between these two words is found in 2 Corinthians 7:10. Literally, "For the sorrow according to God works a *repentance* unto salvation, a *repentance without regret* [negative form of the word for worldly repentance or regret]: but the sorrow of the world [sorrow for failure, not for sin] works out death in the end" (author's italics).

A person can experience worldly sorrow of his own power, brought about by untoward circumstances. But "godly sorrow" or "the sorrow according to God," which works true repentance, is a work of the Holy Spirit.

We have noted that repentance and faith are inseparable graces. Therefore, to the truly repentant sinner the Holy Spirit gives faith whereby he may believe in or commit himself to Christ as Saviour.

John 3:16 follows hard upon Jesus' teaching about the work of the Holy Spirit in regeneration. "Whosoever believeth," therefore, involves the power of the Holy Spirit. This leads such one to experience the birth of the Spirit or the birth from above (John 3:3 ff.). "Except a man be born of water and of the Spirit, he cannot enter into the kingdom of God" (v.5).

"Born of water" has produced many varied interpretations. To say that it refers to baptism is contrary not only to this context but to that of the entire New Testament. Some see it as referring to spiritual cleansing. The author sees it as a reference to the natural birth. But there can be no question about "born of the Spirit." In fact, the entire passage presents a contrast between the natural birth and the spiritual. "That which is born of the flesh [natural birth] is flesh; and that which is born of the Spirit [spiritual birth] is spirit" (v.6).

So in a mystery which is like unto the wind (v.8), in the repentant believer the Holy Spirit works the miracle of the birth from above or regeneration. As the Holy Spirit was the power of conception in the miracle virgin birth of Jesus, so he is the power of God to bring forth a miracle *new creation* in Christ.

Before turning from this matter we note Paul's figure of adoption into the family of God (Rom. 8:14–17; Gal. 4:5–7). This also is a work of the Holy Spirit. Actually there is no conflict between this figure and the birth from above. Jesus, speaking to a

Jew, used the figure of birth; Paul, writing to the church in Rome, used the figure of the Roman law of adoption.

Under this law a slave or a son of one man might be adopted into the family of another. Certain prescribed rules must be met. The price of adoption must be paid. The new father assumed all the debts and obligations of his adopted son. The son, in turn, assumed the obligation of sonship; but he also received the same privileges as did those who were naturally born children. Under Roman law he was regarded as being born into his new family, or being born again. Witnesses were required for the transaction.

A study of the two passages cited above shows how closely Paul paralleled this law in setting forth the Christian experience. For instance, the lost man is in bondage to the flesh and to the law. He is adopted into a new family with a new Father. The price of redemption or adoption is paid.

God has paid all debts and assumed all obligations. The adopted son assumes the obligations of sonship, and receives the privileges or heirship of a son, along with the one who eternally is God's Son. The Holy Spirit is both the power making this possible and the one who witnesses the transaction (Rom. 8:16; Gal. 4:6).

Thus the slave to sin is born again into a new family, into the family of God. Paul presented the legal figure of regeneration; Jesus presented the vital figure of the same experience. And both are wrought by the Holy Spirit.

Sanctification

The New Testament teaches that when a person is regenerated he is *sanctified*. Christians are called "saints," which means "holy ones" or "sanctified ones." For instance, Paul addressed 1 Corinthians thusly: "Unto the church of God which is at Corinth, to them that are sanctified in Christ Jesus, called . . . saints" (1:2). Further reading in this epistle reveals that many of them were not so *saintly* in the popular sense of the word. But they are "called saints." They are "sanctified in Christ Jesus."

We have noted earlier in this volume that the word "holy" or "sanctified" basically had no reference to moral quality. This concept was added to the word as it came to be associated with Jehovah. Its root meaning was that of being dedicated or set apart to the service of a god. In the Judeo-Christian sense it means dedicated to the service of Jehovah.

Unfortunately the modern, popular concept of sanctification is that of sinless perfection. One progressively gets rid of sin until he receives the "second blessing" of the Holy Spirit and is, therefore, sanctified. We have noted in discussing the Holy Spirit in Acts that the New Testament does not teach such. Some who do not hold to the "second blessing" see sanctification as a process whereby one progressively grows into the likeness of Christ. But this also seems to be contrary to the New Testament.

That neither of these ideas explains sanctification is seen in John 17:19. Jesus prayed, "I sanctify myself, that they also might be sanctified through the truth." Jesus had no sin of which to be rid. What he meant was that he dedicated himself to the service of God through the cross, in order that his disciples might also be set apart to God's service through the truth, truth here being synonymous with the gospel of grace (cf. John 1:14,17).

In 1 Corinthians 1:30, Paul says that the Corinthian Christians are "in Christ Jesus, who of God is made unto us wisdom, and righteousness, and sanctification, and redemption." In the Greek text the reading is "wisdom: both righteousness, and sanctification, and full redemption." These three items are involved in the sum total of God's *wisdom in Christ*.

Robertson comments that, though the foundation of the other two, "redemption comes here last for emphasis." [3] The fact is true. But is this the meaning of Paul's order? "Righteousness" involves God's judicial act of declaring the sinner as justified or righteous before him (cf. Rom. 1:17). This act is performed in regeneration. So, is not Paul actually using these three words in their proper order: righteousness or regeneration, sanctification or being set apart to God's service, and full redemption or glorification, the full redemption of both soul and body in heaven (cf. Rom. 8:23; Eph. 1:13-14)?

However, our present emphasis is on the word "sanctification," which is "in Christ Jesus." This calls to mind Paul's word in 1 Corinthians 1:2, the word rendered "are sanctified," a perfect passive participle. The perfect tense means that it was done in the past, it is true in the present, and it will continue to be so in the future. Since they are "sanctified in the sphere of Christ Jesus," this must refer to the moment when they through faith in him came into this sphere. So the experience of sanctification for these *unsaintly* "saints" was in the past, but is also a finished work.

The passive voice of this participle means that the act was performed upon the Corinthian Christians by another. They "are sanctified in the sphere of Christ Jesus." But by whom? The answer is the Holy Spirit. He is the agent in sanctification.

The "holy" Spirit makes "holy" our spirits. Paul speaks of his converts among the Gentiles "being sanctified by the Holy Ghost [Spirit]" (Rom. 15:16). Here again "being sanctified" renders a perfect passive participle. The Thessalonian Christians are said to be chosen of God "to salvation through sanctification of the Spirit and belief of the truth" (2 Thess. 2:13; cf. 1 Cor. 6:11; 1 Peter 1:2; Jude 1). In Hebrews 2:11, sanctification is attributed to Jesus. And Hebrews 10:10 says that "we are sanctified through the offering of the body of Jesus Christ." Here, as in many other places, the work of Jesus and of the Holy Spirit are so closely related they appear as one. But the overall teaching is that sanctification is made possible through the redemptive work of Christ. It occurs "in the sphere of Christ Jesus," but it is effected by the Holy Spirit.

Is sanctification an instantaneous act or is it a process? It would appear from the preceding study that it is an instantaneous act which results in a process. When a person is regenerated, the Holy Spirit takes up his abode in that life. Jesus said that the world cannot receive the Spirit "because it seeth him not, neither knoweth him: but ye know him; for he dwelleth with you, and shall be in you" (John 14:17). Thenceforth, the body of the Christian becomes the temple of the Holy Spirit (cf. 1 Cor. 6:19). Thus the Christian is sanctified or set apart to the service of God.

However, even though sanctification is an instantaneous act, the believer should grow in that state of sanctification (cf. 2 Peter 3:18). This thought is involved in the terms used for becoming a Christian: the birth from above and the figure of discipleship. The moment that one is born of the Spirit he is a child of God. But he grows and develops in that relationship. Likewise, the moment one becomes a disciple he is a pupil of Christ. In that relationship he grows in knowledge and skill. Of course, sanctification does not mean that one will automatically do these things. Sanctification is an arbitrary act of the Holy Spirit based upon one's receiving Christ as Saviour. Growth in the state of sanctification is likewise a work of the Holy Spirit, but it also involves the submissive will of the Christian (cf. Rom. 6:6–13; Heb. 5:11 to 6:3).

The goal of sanctification might well be stated in the words of Ephesians 4:1–16. Paul exhorts his readers to "walk worthy [worthily] of the vocation [calling] wherewith ye are called" (v.1). "Worthily" renders an adverb which carries the idea of weight. On one side of the scales you put your calling as a Christian. On the other side you put your manner of life as a Christian. The latter should balance the former. A marvelous passage follows, in which Paul cites the work of the Father, Son, and Spirit in the Christian. This work is "for the edifying of the body of Christ: Till we all come in [into] the unity of the faith, and of the [full] knowledge of the Son of God, unto a perfect [complete, adult] man, unto the measure of the stature of the fulness of Christ: . . . speaking the truth in love, may grow up into him in all things, which is the head, even Christ: . . . maketh increase of the body unto the edifying of itself in love" (vv.12–16).

Thus, by the power of the Holy Spirit we can say with John, "Beloved, now are we the sons of God, and it doth not yet appear what we shall be: but we know that, when he shall appear, we shall be like him; for we shall see him as he is" (1 John 3:2).

Glorification

The goal of full redemption is the Christian's sum total of reward in heaven. This involves the redemption of both the soul, life, and body—the last coming at the final resurrection from the dead. Paul speaks of this as "a spiritual body" or a body controlled by the Spirit (1 Cor. 15:44). He further says that it will be fashioned after the glorious body of the Lord Jesus Christ (Phil. 3:21).

By the redemption of "life" we mean the Christian life or the life which we live in the state of sanctification. The Bible teaches degrees of reward in heaven. This is inferred in Jesus' parables of the talents and of the judgment (cf. Matt. 25). Furthermore, Paul speaks of those who build upon the foundation of Christ (1 Cor. 3:10 ff.). Some build with gold, silver, and precious stones; others use wood, hay, and stubble. The judgment shall reveal the material used in each case, as a fire reveals dependability. "If any man's work abide . . . he shall receive a reward. If any man's work shall be burned, he shall suffer loss: but he himself shall be saved; yet so as by fire" (vv.14–15). Suffice it to say, each saved person will enjoy heaven to the extent of his ability; but the ability of one will be greater than the ability of another. This provides an incentive to develop in the state of sanctification. Paul gives the added incentive that both the individual Christian and the church are the temple of the Holy Spirit whose work it is not only to sanctify but to develop us (1 Cor. 3:16; 6:19). Thus he provides for us a greater hope of glory.

There are many references to glorification which make no specific mention of the Holy Spirit. But in this as in many other matters the work of the Spirit is intermingled with that of the Father and the Son. This work is still performed through the power of the Spirit of God sent forth to do the work of God.

This intermingling of work is clearly seen in Romans 8. Paul says that "the law of the Spirit of life in Christ Jesus hath made me free from the law of sin and death" (v.2). Furthermore, "If the Spirit of him that raised up Jesus from the dead dwell in you, he that raised up Christ from the dead shall also quicken your mortal bodies by his Spirit that dwelleth in you" (v.11).

Then follows that wonderful passage about being adopted into the family of God, whereby we being led of the Spirit become sons of God, "and if children, then heirs; heirs of God, and joint-heirs with Christ; *if so be that we suffer with him, that we may be also glorified together*" (v.17, author's italics). In other words, the degree of our glory with Christ in heaven will correspond to the degree of our suffering with him on earth. But the suffering fades into insignificance when compared "with the glory which shall be revealed in us" (v.18).

This glory will involve a redeemed universe, redeemed souls, and redeemed bodies (vv.19–23). "Not only they, but ourselves also, which have the firstfruits of the Spirit, even we ourselves groan within ourselves, waiting for the adoption, to wit, the redemption of our body" (v.23).

In our waiting the Holy Spirit is our ever-present helper, even to putting words to our sighs which cannot be uttered (vv.26–27). Thus we can know that God through his Spirit works in all things for good to those who love him, and who are the called according to his purpose (v.28). For "whom he did predestinate, them he also called: and whom he called, them he also justified: and whom he justified, them he also glorified" (v.30). Truly, we are not left as orphans in the world, for through his Holy Spirit God will preserve and enable to persevere those who are regenerated and sanctified unto his unfailing goal—our glorification.

Perseverance of the Saints

This treatment of the Holy Spirit in evangelism would be incomplete without dealing with the perseverance of the saints. Many New Testament passages teach this sublime truth. But two specific words used in connection with the Holy Spirit call for our attention. These words are "seal" and "earnest."

In Ephesians 1:13-14 Paul says, "In whom [Christ] ye also trusted, after that he heard the word of truth, the gospel of your salvation: in whom also after that ye believed, ye were *sealed* with that holy Spirit of promise, which is the *earnest* of our inheritance until [unto] the [full] redemption of the purchased possession" (author's italics). These figures are also found in 2 Corinthians 1:22; 5:5; and Ephesians 4:30.

Both of these terms are drawn from the commercial life of that day. A *seal* was a mark of ownership. For instance, a seal from the signet ring of a king marked the sealed object as belonging to the king. So the Holy Spirit in the Christian's life is God's seal of ownership. None other dares to tamper with it.

The picture is even clearer with regard to *earnest*. This word was used of earnest money, or a down payment for a thing purchased. This word appears in the New Testament only three times, and each time in connection with the Holy Spirit. He is God's "earnest money" to guarantee that God will fulfil his agreement to save all who come to Christ in faith. Each redeemed soul is God's purchased possession. Recalling the threefold nature of salvation as regeneration, sanctification, and glorification, this thought enables us to understand the use of the word "earnest."

Paul speaks of the "full redemption of the purchased possession." In Christ's death on the cross God purchased your soul as
his possession. The fulness of the transaction involved the redemption of both soul, life, and body, or the full redemption in heaven.
Regeneration and sanctification are accomplished facts when one
receives Christ as Saviour. But there yet remains the full redemption or glorification in heaven. So, when one becomes a Christian,
God indwells his life in the Holy Spirit. And the Holy Spirit is
God's earnest money to guarantee that he will complete the transaction.

In business practice, if the purchaser goes through with the
agreement, the earnest money becomes a part of the purchase
payment. But if he does not go through with it, he loses his earnest
money.

Now what does this say to us? Paul says that God has *put up*
his Holy Spirit as earnest money to guarantee that he will go
through with his agreement to save eternally those who trust in
Jesus. The Holy Spirit is God. So in effect God has *put up* himself
as the guarantee. He has staked his very being on honoring his
promise to save to the uttermost those who believe in his Son. If
he fails to do so, he loses his earnest money. He loses himself! Who
can fear with such security as that?

We close this chapter on a beautiful and romantic note. In the
papyri this word rendered "earnest" is used for "the engagement
ring." In this light, therefore, may we not say in truth that the
Holy Spirit is "the engagement ring" which the bridegroom gives
to his bride, looking toward the marriage feast of the Lamb?
When the bridegroom shall appear may we, through the Holy
Spirit, truly be "prepared as a bride adorned for her husband"
(Rev. 21:2)!

The Spread of the Gospel

The Holy Spirit has been called the administrator of the Godhead. He is the Spirit of God sent forth to do the work of God. In the Old Testament we have seen how in creation he brought order out of chaos. He also enabled certain individuals to perform given tasks for God, ranging all the way from mighty deliverances to the skills necessary to construct the tabernacle and its various accouterments of worship. He inspired and illuminated the prophets for their ministry.

In the New Testament the picture continues. Throughout the four Gospels the Spirit is seen as working with and through Jesus in every phase of his ministry. The administrative work of the Spirit is evident at various points in the Epistles and in the Revelation.

However, it is in the book of Acts that the Holy Spirit's role as administrator is most clearly depicted. For it is here that he is seen specifically continuing that which Jesus "began both to do and teach" (1:1).

The purpose of this chapter is to retrace our steps through Acts with a view to noting the administrative aspects of the Holy Spirit's work in the spread of the gospel throughout the Roman world. In so doing we shall have occasion to touch upon certain previously treated passages. However, there will be a different emphasis.

Pentecost

The prophecy of Joel had foreseen the time when the Holy Spirit would come upon the people of God for a special ministry. On the night before his death Jesus anticipated the time beyond his ascension when his followers would carry out his various commissions to preach the gospel for the kingdom. And he promised them the abiding presence of the Holy Spirit to empower and guide them in this enterprise. In Jerusalem, shortly before his ascension, he commanded them to delay the launching of this endeavor until they should get themselves clothed with power from on high (Luke 24:49; Acts 1:4).

Finally, just before Jesus was taken up from them, he said, "But ye shall receive power, after that the Holy Ghost [Spirit] is come upon you: and ye shall be witnesses unto me both in Jerusalem, and in all Judaea, and in Samaria, and unto the uttermost part of the earth" (Acts 1:8).

We have already touched upon Luke's purpose in writing the book of Acts.[1] One suggested purpose is to record the spread of the gospel throughout the Roman Empire, with Acts 1:8 forming the outline. Of course, there are some areas of this empire which do not figure in Acts, so this cannot fully explain the purpose of the book. Nevertheless, it is quite clear that that which follows is in measure fashioned according to this verse. Certainly the disciples did begin in Jerusalem and did spread southward, northward, and westward. Their ministry carried them to certain points in Judea, Samaria, and "unto the uttermost part of the earth." To the ancients this last phrase described Spain on the western edge of the empire. Paul expressed his intention of going to Spain (Rom. 15:24,28). Acts ends with Paul in Rome.

Some suggest that Luke intended writing a sequel to Acts in which he would record such a Spanish ministry, perhaps following Paul to his death in Rome following a second Roman imprisonment. But this is only surmise. Certain references in Paul's latest epistles suggest that he may have gone to Spain after his first Roman imprisonment. But this cannot be proved.

However, we do know that Acts records the spread of the gospel from Jerusalem to Rome. And in this record the Holy Spirit is seen directing or authenticating this movement at given stages.

At Pentecost the promise of the coming of the Holy Spirit in power was fulfilled (Acts 2:1 ff.). Since we have already dwelt upon this, it is sufficient only to note here that this experience transformed the disciples from a fearful, uncertain band into a fearless, purposeful army which boldly stormed the citadels of evil in a hostile world. Truly they were not left as orphans. Jesus had come to them in the person of the Holy Spirit. And while at times uncertainty dogged their footsteps, under the guidance of the Holy Spirit they overcame all obstacles. In him they were sufficient for the task.

Persecution

Following Pentecost, the first administrative mission of the Holy Spirit was within the Christian community in Jerusalem. We have seen how he guided them in the settling of certain problems which arose within the fellowship itself (Acts 5:1 ff.; 6:1 ff.). But his greatest ministry at this point was to sustain them in their relationship with the hostile Jewish community about them. He was their helper during the wave of persecution which swirled about them. Jesus had promised such a ministry (cf. Matt. 10:19–20; John 14:16–18). And they found that the promise was true.

The first persecution came as the result of Peter's healing of a lame man at the gate of the Temple called Beautiful (Acts 3:1 ff.). Seeing this miracle, an evidence of the power of the Holy Spirit, the people in amazement came to Peter and John on Solomon's porch (v.11). To them Peter preached a sermon in which he boldly charged his hearers with the death of Jesus. "But ye denied the Holy One and the Just, and desired a murderer [Barabbas] to be granted unto you; and killed the Prince of life, whom God hath raised from the dead; whereof we are witnesses" (vv.14–15; cf. John 15:26–27). Then he called upon them to repent and be converted.

Even as Peter was preaching, certain priests, including some Sadducees, came upon them. They were indignant because Peter was preaching "through Jesus the resurrection from the dead" (4:2). This was a double insult to them, for they had reported that Jesus' dead body had been stolen from the tomb. To preach the resurrection, especially that of Jesus, was contrary to the basic belief of the Sadducees. So they arrested the two apostles.

The following day they were brought before the Sanhedrin (vv.5 ff.). When asked by what name or power they had performed the miracle of the previous day, they received more answer than they wanted. Jesus' promise was fulfilled as before this *council* the Holy Spirit spoke through Peter:

Be it known unto you all, and to all the people of Israel, that by the name of Jesus Christ of Nazareth, whom ye crucified, whom God raised from the dead, even by him doth this man stand here before you whole. . . . Neither is there salvation in any other: for there is none other name under heaven given among men, whereby we must be saved (4:10–12).

The Sanhedrin was no match for the Holy Spirit. Neither could the rulers of the people and the elders of Israel deny the miracle which was evident before them. They could only threaten the apostles and command them to cease such preaching and teaching. But still the Holy Spirit spoke through the apostles. They had fled from danger in Gethsemane. But no more. Both Peter and John answered, "Whether it be right in the sight of God to hearken unto you more than unto God, judge ye. For we cannot but speak the things which we have seen and heard" (vv. 19–20). They had seen the fact with their eyes. They had heard its meaning from both Jesus and the Holy Spirit (cf. John 16:13–14). So with the Sanhedrin's threats falling upon unheeding ears, the apostles were set free. The Holy Spirit had not failed them.

Upon returning to their fellow Christians they related their experience, and with one accord they prayed to God (vv.24 ff.). They did not ask to be free from persecution: "Now, Lord, behold their threatenings: and grant unto thy servants, that with all boldness they may speak thy word" (v.29). And their prayer received an immediate answer. The Spirit manifested his presence and power as the house was shaken: "They were all filled with the Holy Ghost [Spirit], and they spake the word of God with boldness" (v.31). Instead of persecution shaking their resolve, it, by the Holy Spirit, served only to solidify their *koinōnia* or fellowship (vv.32 ff.).

Following the tragic fate of Ananias and Sapphira in falsifying the Holy Spirit, many miracles were performed by the Spirit-filled apostles. Consequently the wrath of the Sanhedrin once again fell upon the Christians (5:17 ff.). All of the apostles were imprisoned. But an angel (messenger) of the Lord delivered them, and sent them back to the Temple to preach. Arrested again, they were brought before the Jewish authorities who reminded them of their order not to preach. For their trouble they received another sermon (vv.29–32). The answer of the Sanhedrin was that they "took counsel to slay them" (v.33).

At this point help came from an unexpected source. The famed teacher Gamaliel reasoned that they should not continue the persecution (vv.34 ff.). Citing incidents of false messiahs, he concluded, "Refrain from these men, and let them alone: for if this counsel or this work be of men, it will come to nought: but if it be of God, ye cannot overthrow it; lest haply ye be found even to fight against God" (Acts 5:38–39).

Strange instruments of the Holy Spirit! An angel and a renowned

Jewish teacher. But he fulfilled his mission as helper, for the Sanhedrin merely beat the apostles and renewed their order not to preach. What was the effect upon the apostles? They rejoiced that they were worthy to suffer for Jesus. "Daily in the temple, and in every house, they ceased not to teach and preach Jesus Christ" (v.42). Truly, the persecutors could not overcome this work, for it was the work of God through his Holy Spirit.

The next follower of Jesus to face persecution was Stephen, a deacon. "Full of faith and power," he worked many miracles among the people (6:8). This brought him into conflict with the members of certain synagogues who debated with him, "and they were not able to resist the wisdom and the spirit by which he spake" (v.10).

In answer to false accusations, brought against him before the Sanhedrin, Stephen delivered a masterful sermon, rehearsing the history of Israel (7:2 ff.). The running refrain was that always Israel had rejected the leaders whom God had sent to her. Once again the Holy Spirit spoke through a persecuted Christian. Finally, Stephen concluded, "Ye stiffnecked and uncircumcised in heart and ears, ye do always resist the Holy Ghost [Spirit]: as your fathers did, so do ye" (v.51).

At the moment when the Jews were at the point of doing him bodily harm, the Holy Spirit enabled Stephen to see into heaven (vv.55–56). There he "saw the glory of God, and Jesus standing on the right hand of God" (v.55). Is there any peculiar significance in the fact that Jesus was *standing?* Hebrews 10:12 says that following his earthly ministry Jesus "sat down on the right hand of God." Now the first time thereafter that he is seen by Spirit-enlightened human eyes, he is standing. Does this suggest the eager attention with which Jesus witnessed this scene, when one of his followers is about to become the first Christian martyr? Or, was he standing to welcome this martyr home? Certainly these are suggestive thoughts.

Whatever else may be drawn from this scene, it is evident that by the Holy Spirit Stephen knew that he did not suffer alone and unknown to his Lord, for he said, "Behold, I see the heavens opened, and the Son of man standing on the right hand of God" (Acts 7:56). For this he paid with his life, as he was stoned to death, all the while praying for his executioners.

But he did not die in vain, for a young man named Saul saw him die. And he never got away from the sight, for in his heart the Holy Spirit planted a seed which was to bear abundant fruit.

Up to this time, since Pentecost, the witness of the Christians had been confined to Jerusalem. But following the death of Stephen there arose a great persecution under the leadership of Saul (8:1–4). This resulted in the scattering of the Christian community, except the apostles, throughout Judea and Samaria. "Therefore they that were scattered abroad went every where preaching the word" (v.4).

The Holy Spirit certainly did not cause the persecution. But he worked in it for good to those who loved God and who were fitted into his purpose. He helped the persecuted. Even when Stephen was martyred, he used it for kingdom gain. And he emboldened those who were scattered abroad to continue to preach the gospel. In every sense he fulfilled the promise of Jesus that he would be helper and guide to the Christian community in its time of need.

Missions

As the gospel moved out of Jerusalem into Judea, Samaria, and beyond, we see the Holy Spirit directing the mighty sweep of missions. He gave encouragement, authenticated new developments, helped in enlisting new recruits, guided the church as it wrestled with doctrinal problems, and was ever in the midst of the fray. Like a mighty army moved the church of God.

One of the greatest barriers in the spread of the gospel in the early years following Pentecost was not persecution but religious

and racial prejudice. The Holy Spirit struggled mightily to produce a climate in which the gospel might be preached "unhinderedly."

The first step in this movement involved preaching the gospel
to *Samaritans* or half Jews. The Gospels reveal the strong antag-
onism between the Jews and the Samaritans. Up to this point only
Jesus himself had stepped over this barrier (cf. John 4).

It was quite a development, therefore, when Philip, driven from
Jerusalem, preached the gospel in the city of Samaria (8:5 ff.). A
great revival resulted, and many souls were saved. When word of
this reached the apostles in Jerusalem, they sent Peter and John
to investigate. Upon arriving and praying for these new converts,
they laid their hands on them, "and they received the Holy Ghost
[Spirit]" (v.17). There is no mention of an ecstatic evidence of
this. But in some manner the Holy Spirit manifested himself. In
short, his coming upon these Samaritan Christians was his authen-
tication of the preaching of the gospel to them. The apostles recognized this fact, because on their way back to Jerusalem, they
"preached the gospel in many villages of the Samaritans" (v.25).

An interesting interlude occurred in Samaria. Simon, a sorcerer,
is said to have believed and been baptized, along with other
Samaritans (v.13). Evidently he did not believe in Jesus. He
merely believed the evidence of the miracles which Philip wrought.
So, when he saw the converts receive the Holy Spirit at the hands
of the apostles, he decided that this was greater than any of his
tricks of sorcery. Therefore, he sought to buy this power for himself. But Peter strongly rebuked him, saying that the power of the
Holy Spirit was not for sale. From this incident there came into our
language the term "simony," the act of trying to barter in spiritual
things. No, the Holy Spirit's power is not for sale, but it is available to all who come to Jesus in faith.

The next departure in preaching the gospel was to a *Jewish
proselyte,* the Ethiopian eunuch. Some would argue that he was

not a proselyte because he was a eunuch, and that no mutilated person could be one.[2] Whether or not this man be regarded as a true proselyte, his was certainly a new development in the spread of the gospel. For he was neither a Jew nor a Samaritan.

This development came about through an express command of the Holy Spirit. For an angel of the Lord told Philip to leave Samaria and to go to a lonely road which led from Jerusalem to Gaza (8:26 ff.). There he encountered "a man of Ethiopia, an eunuch of great authority under Candace queen of the Ethiopians, who had the charge of all her treasure" (v.27). He had been to Jerusalem to worship. So, even if he were not a proselyte, he certainly was an adherent to the Jewish faith. He was reading from the roll of Isaiah 53. Was this by chance? Or, was it the guidance of the Holy Spirit? Certainly no better passage could have provided Philip a basis from which to preach "unto him Jesus" (v.35).

As the chariot approached, "The Spirit said unto Philip, Go near, and join thyself to this chariot" (v. 29). This resulted in this Holy-Spirit-led "hitchhiker" winning this Ethiopian to Christ. After his baptism the eunuch went on his way rejoicing. In all likelihood the Holy Spirit used him to plant the gospel in Ethiopia, a land which subsequently had a very strong Christian movement.

His mission accomplished, the Holy Spirit caught Philip away, and he continued to preach the gospel along the Mediterranean coast until he came to Caesarea (v.40).

There is no greater event in the spread of the gospel in the first century, or in any other for that matter, than the *conversion of Saul of Tarsus* (9:1 ff.). The Holy Spirit never let him get away from the impression made on him by the death of Stephen. Even his *war-horse* persecution probably was greatly motivated by his *kicking against the pricks* of conviction (cf. v.5). At any rate, while on a mission of persecution to Damascus, suddenly in a blinding light at midday Jesus himself appeared to Saul (vv. 3 ff.). This resulted in his conversion.

Later, in Damascus, at the hand of Ananias he was filled with the Holy Spirit (v.17). Thus the Holy Spirit authenticated this drastic change in one who was the dreaded scourge of the Christians. This haughty Pharisee became a "chosen vessel" of the Lord to bear his name before Gentiles, kings, and the children of Israel (v.15). This bloodthirsty, persecuting rabbi became a bloodshedding, persecuted apostle of the Lord. He became the greatest of all trophies of the convicting and transforming power of the Holy Spirit.

The gospel reached farther out as through Peter, one of the most Hebraic of the apostles, the Holy Spirit preached to Cornelius, "a devout man, and one that feared God with all his house" (10:2). He was a Roman centurion stationed at Caesarea. Now Cornelius was a *God-fearer*. He was a Gentile who was interested in the Jewish religion, but who had not yet become a Jewish proselyte. He was a generous man toward the poor "and prayed to God alway." During such a period of prayer, the Holy Spirit gave him a vision in which an angel of the Lord told him to send to nearby Joppa to get Peter to come and instruct him as to what to do.

The next day in Joppa the Holy Spirit gave Peter a vision which prepared him to answer the summons of Cornelius (vv. 9–16). When messengers from the centurion arrived, Peter went with them and preached in Cornelius' house (vv.24 ff.). This within itself was quite a step for Peter. It was possible only through the Holy Spirit.

What strange sounding words fell from his lips as he began his sermon! "Of a truth I perceive that God is no respecter of persons: but in every nation he that feareth him, and worketh righteousness, is accepted with him" (vv.34–35). Then he preached unto them Jesus, calling upon his listeners to receive remission of sins through faith in him (v.43).

Evidently they responded immediately, for "while Peter yet spake these words, the Holy Ghost [Spirit] fell on all them which heard the word" (v.44). The Christian Jews who had accompanied Peter were astonished that the Holy Spirit had come even upon Gentiles. But he had done so, as he placed his approval upon this mission to God-fearers. Here those who had received the Holy Spirit spoke in tongues as they magnified God. This suggests that the Holy Spirit gave an even greater evidence of his presence to the preaching of the gospel to God-fearing Gentiles than to the preaching to the Samaritans or to Saul. Such a demonstration was necessary for so drastic a departure from Jewish custom (cf. vv. 47–48).

Upon his return to Jerusalem Peter was in trouble with his Jewish brethren (11:1 ff.). They accused him of entering the home of a Gentile and of eating with him. But Peter rehearsed the entire matter to them, saying that he had acted under the express orders of the Holy Spirit (v.12).

Telling of the coming of the Spirit upon them as upon the Christians at Pentecost, he recalled John the Baptist's promise that Jesus would baptize with the Holy Spirit. Then he drove home his clincher argument: "Forasmuch then as God gave them the like gift as he did unto us, who believed on the Lord Jesus Christ; what was I, that I could withstand God?" (v.17). This settled the matter. For the former critics now joined in praise (v.18).

The gospel continued to spread, so that finally certain disciples came to Antioch far to the north (11:19 ff.). Here they found certain *pagan Greeks* to whom they preached the Lord Jesus, "and a great number believed, and turned unto the Lord" (v.21). This marked a new development in the Christian enterprise. Heretofore the gospel had been preached to Jews, half Jews, a Jewish proselyte (?), and to God-fearers. All of these had some connection with the Jewish faith. But in Antioch, for the first time in Acts, the gospel was proclaimed to purely Gentile pagans. And they also had been saved.

So when this startling word reached Jerusalem, the church

there sent one of its most trusted men, Barnabas, to investigate
the matter (v.22; cf. 4:36–37; 9:27). He is described as "a good
man, and full of the Holy Ghost [Spirit] and of faith" (11:24).
This Holy Spirit-led man saw that the conversion of these pagan
Gentiles was genuine—so much so that he added his own ministry
to the others, "and much people was added unto the Lord."

So great was the revival that broke out there that Barnabas
brought Saul from Tarsus to help him. For a "whole year they
assembled themselves with the church, and taught much people.
And the disciples were called Christians first in Antioch" (vv.
25–26).

During these days the Holy Spirit gave to the brethren in Judea
proof positive that the conversion of Gentiles was genuine. One of
the Christians of Antioch "signified by the Spirit" that a great
dearth would come throughout the Roman Empire. So the disciples at Antioch sent relief to the Christians in Judea. When
Barnabas and Saul arrived in Jerusalem with this gift, they bore
tangible evidence that the Holy Spirit had effected a *koinōnia*
even between Christians of Jewish and Gentile backgrounds.

By this time the gospel had spread throughout Palestine. Therefore, the Holy Spirit led in an entirely new departure. The gospel
must now be proclaimed in Asia Minor. So the Holy Spirit said to
the church in Antioch, "Separate me Barnabas and Saul for the
work whereunto I have called them" (13:2). "So they, being sent
forth by the Holy Ghost [Spirit], departed unto Seleucia; and from
thence they sailed to Cyprus" (v.4). From there they sailed to
Asia Minor where they preached in Perga in Pamphylia, Antioch
in Pisidia, Iconium, Lystra, and Derbe.

Throughout this ministry the Holy Spirit authenticated this new
work. He came upon the disciples at Antioch in Pisidia (13:14).
In both Iconium and Derbe he worked miracles through his witnesses (14:3,8–10). So evident was the Holy Spirit's power in
this mission that when Saul, now called Paul (cf. 13:9), and

Barnabas returned to Antioch in Syria they reported to the church "how [that] he [God] had opened the door of faith unto the Gentiles" (14:27).

One phase of the administrative work of the Holy Spirit had to do with *doctrine*. Jesus had said that he would teach and guide into all truth. The element of truth implies the possibility of error. The spread of the gospel among the Gentiles created a doctrinal problem. We have seen the hesitancy on the part of the church in Jerusalem to accept the fact that non-Jews as such could be saved. But in every case the Holy Spirit had authenticated the fact. Nevertheless, there was an element in Jerusalem which insisted that before Gentiles could be saved they must first become Jews, then believe on Jesus for salvation. These people were called Judaizers. Certain of them came from Judea to Antioch, saying, "Except ye be circumcised after the manner of Moses, ye cannot be saved" (15:1; cf. v.5).

Paul and Barnabas challenged them in heated debate. The issue was whether Gentiles could be saved by grace through faith, or whether they were to be saved by works plus faith. When the problem was not resolved, it was determined that Paul, Barnabas, and others should bring the matter before the apostles and elders in Jerusalem (v.2). While it is not specifically stated, we may assume that this decision was reached under the guidance of the Holy Spirit.

Paul records this meeting in Jerusalem in Galatians 2. In chapter 1 he insisted that he received his gospel not from men but by a direct revelation from the Lord (1:6 ff.). Luke's account of this meeting is found in Acts 15.

The debate continued in Jerusalem (v.5). Finally, Peter rehearsed his experience in the house of Cornelius (vv.7–11). He noted how the Holy Spirit had confirmed this ministry. Then he concluded, "Now therefore why tempt ye God, to put a yoke upon the neck of the disciples, which neither our fathers nor we were able to bear? *But we believe that through the grace of the Lord Jesus Christ we shall be saved, even as they"* (vv.10–11, author's italics). Thus he declared that instead of Gentiles' being saved as Jews, even the Jews must be saved in the same way as Gentiles are saved. This is a distinctive landmark in the struggle for an unhindered gospel.

Paul and Barnabas added their word as to how the Holy Spirit through "miracles and wonders" had wrought among the Gentiles (v.12). Then James, the pastor of the Jerusalem church, spoke to the effect that this ministry among the Gentiles was a fulfilment of prophecy (vv.14–18). "Wherefore my sentence is, that we trouble not them, which from among the Gentiles are turned to God" (v.19). This settled the matter insofar as the assembly was concerned, even though the Judaizers continued to preach this gospel of works plus faith.

However, the decision of the body was written in a letter, sent by men chosen by the church, along with Paul and Barnabas, to the "brethren which are of the Gentiles in Antioch and Syria and Cilicia" (v.23). The church in Jerusalem had not commanded the Judaizers to teach their doctrine of works plus faith (v.24). After commending Barnabas and Paul, they wrote their decision in the matter: *"It seemed good to the Holy Ghost [Spirit], and to us,* to lay upon you no greater burden than these necessary things" (v.28, author's italics). Note "to the Holy Spirit, and to us." They recognized that the Holy Spirit had led them in their deliberations. Thus they refused to require Gentiles to become proselytes before believing in Jesus. Salvation is by grace through faith apart from the works of the law. But they did admonish these Gentile Christians to abstain from pagan practices (v.29).

Thus was made one of the greatest doctrinal decisions in Christian history. And it was made under the Spirit's guidance.

Following this clear unleashing of the gospel from the fetters of Jewish legalism, things moved rapidly. Paul and Silas revisited some of the cities in Asia Minor where the gospel had been planted during the first missionary journey (16:1 ff.). Ephesus, in the Roman province of Asia, was the principal city in Asia Minor, so apparently Paul had thought to go there to inaugurate a work. But the Holy Spirit had other plans for the present. With the gospel firmly planted in Palestine, Syria, and Asia Minor, it was the Spirit's purpose to launch a campaign *to conquer Europe.*

But when Paul sought to go southward to Ephesus he was "forbidden of the Holy Ghost [Spirit] to preach the word in Asia" (v.6). Assaying them to go northward into Bithynia, "the Spirit suffered them not" (v.7). How the Holy Spirit did these things is not stated. It may have been by outward circumstances or by inward impressions. However it was, the Holy Spirit guided Paul and his company by Mysia to Troas (v.8). This was a port on the Aegean Sea across from Neapolis and Philippi in Macedonia on the continent of Europe. At Troas the Spirit gave Paul a vision of a man from Macedonia, saying, "Come over into Macedonia, and help us" (v.9). So from Troas they crossed over into Europe.

We need but sketch briefly the events which followed. Following a supernatural deliverance from prison in Philippi (vv.25 ff.), persecution in Thessalonica (17:1 ff.), a kind reception in Berea (vv.10–12) but forced to leave in the face of Jewish opposition, they finally came to Athens. In Athens Paul preached one of his greatest sermons to the philosophers (vv.22 ff.). Some would call this sermon a failure, but it resulted in the conversion of a member of the group on the Areopagus, a woman of prominence, and others. This was the small beginning of what was to become a great work in Athens. Nevertheless, Paul was laughed out of Athens, and from there went to the prosperous but wicked city of Corinth.

When the Jewish community in Corinth refused to heed Paul,

he turned to the Gentiles (18:6). He had had rough treatment since coming to Europe. Perhaps he wondered if this mission was within the Lord's will. It was at this point that in a vision the Lord said to him, "Be not afraid, but speak, and hold not thy peace: For I am with thee, and no man shall set on thee to hurt thee: for I have much people in this city" (vv.9–10).

Again the Holy Spirit authenticated a new phase of the spread of the kingdom. Thus encouraged, Paul had a fruitful ministry of eighteen months in Corinth (v.11).

Finally, from Corinth Paul did go to Ephesus (19:1 ff.), where for two years he had a successful ministry (v.10). There the Holy Spirit came upon the converted disciples of John the Baptist, and, by the power of the Holy Spirit, Paul worked many miracles (vv.11 ff.). On a later visit, Paul exhorted the elders of the church, "Take heed therefore unto yourselves [elders], and to all the flock, over the which the Holy Ghost [Spirit] hath made you overseers [bishops], to feed [as a shepherd or pastor] the church of God" (20:28). Note the three terms, elder, bishop, and pastor, used to refer to one office.[3] But the point of emphasis here is that they were appointed to this office by the Holy Spirit. In various ways, therefore, the work of the Holy Spirit as administrator is seen in the mission in Ephesus.

One final example remains as to the administrative work of the Holy Spirit—*Paul's mission to Rome*. Actually this mission was rooted in an impression of the Spirit in the apostle's heart while he was in Corinth (Rom. 15:23) and later in Ephesus (Acts 19:21). First, he must go to Jerusalem, for it was thereby that the Spirit purposed to take him to Rome. To the Ephesian elders he said, "Now, behold, I go bound in the spirit [Spirit] unto Jerusalem, . . . the Holy Ghost [Spirit] witnesseth in every city, saying that bonds and afflictions abide me" (20:22–23). But these things were necessary that he might fulfil his ministry (v.24).

And then a very strange thing happened. On his way to Jerusalem Paul arrived at the house of Philip the evangelist in Caesarea (21:8). While there a prophet named Agabus from Judea came to visit Paul. Using Paul's girdle, the prophet bound his own hands and feet. Then he said, "Thus saith the Holy Ghost [Spirit], So shall the Jews at Jerusalem bind the man that owneth this girdle, and shall deliver him into the hands of the Gentiles" (v.11). Hearing this, Paul's friends sought to dissuade him from going to Jerusalem. But he insisted, saying, "I am ready not to be bound only, but also to die at Jerusalem for the name of the Lord Jesus" (v.13). Whereupon the people said, "The will of the Lord be done" (v.14).

There are those who see in Agabus' action an effort on the part of the Holy Spirit to warn Paul to avoid Jerusalem, and that his refusal to take the warning resulted in his subsequent imprisonment. But this misses the entire point. The Spirit was simply revealing to Paul here, as on previous occasions, that which awaited him. But Paul knew the mind of the Spirit, and he was willing to die, if necessary, to do his will.

Paul did spend two years in prison in Caesarea. But the record shows how the Holy Spirit protected and guided him as he preached the gospel before governors and a king. Finally, seeing that he would receive no justice before the corrupt governors in Caesarea, he exercised his right as a Roman citizen to appeal to Caesar (25:11-12). Not only did the Holy Spirit propose to send him to Rome but to place him before the Roman Caesar himself. Judging by the apostle's deportment before Felix and Festus, we may well imagine that Nero himself heard the gospel from this prisoner. Only thus could the gospel have come to the highest tribunal in the empire.

Festus said, "Hast thou appealed unto Caesar? unto Caesar shalt thou go" (v.12). So, finally, Paul began his long voyage to Rome. In a storm at sea it seemed that all was lost, but in the darkest hour the apostle encouraged the entire complement of the ship, saying that no person would be lost, only the ship (27:22). "For there stood by me this night the angel of God, whose I am, and whom I serve, saying, Fear not, Paul; thou must be brought before Caesar: and, lo, God hath given thee all them that sail with thee. Wherefore, sirs, be of good cheer: for I believe God, that it shall be even as it was told me" (vv.23–25). Even the winds and waves could not defeat the purpose of the Holy Spirit.

Finally, when Paul arrived in Rome, he sent for the leading Jews of the city (28:17 ff.). He would give them the opportunity of heeding the gospel. But when some of them hardened their hearts against it, Paul said, "Well spake the Holy Ghost [Spirit] by Esaias the prophet unto our fathers, saying, Go unto this people, and say, Hearing ye shall hear, and shall not understand; and seeing ye shall see, and not perceive: for the heart of this people is waxed gross, and their ears are dull of hearing, and their eyes have they closed; . . . Be it known therefore unto you, that the salvation of God is sent unto the Gentiles, and that they will hear it" (vv.25–28).

"Paul dwelt two whole years in his own hired house, and received all that came in unto him, preaching the kingdom of God, and teaching those things which concern the Lord Jesus Christ, with all confidence, no man forbidding him" (vv.30–31).

Thus through the administration of the Holy Spirit we have an "unhindered" gospel. May we preach it through the power which he gives to us!

Specific Ministries

One of the major functions of the Holy Spirit was and is to empower and guide the followers of Jesus in performing the work of the kingdom. In this function the Spirit bestowed certain gifts upon certain people to enable them to perform specific ministries. These gifts were not given for the personal glory of any individual, but for the essential functions of the body of believers. In some cases, for instance Paul, a single individual might receive several gifts. A person's ability was in one sense a gift of the Holy Spirit.

The sense of "gifts" as used in the New Testament involves more. In the more prosaic sense it might involve the heightening of some natural endowment. But more likely "gifts" or charismata (grace gifts) involved special enduements. We shall see that in most instances these gifts were temporary in nature.

Strange to say, the most complete discussion of these gifts in the New Testament stems from the abuse of them by the members of the church in Corinth. Therefore, our present treatment will center largely in 1 Corinthians 12–14. For in this passage Paul endeavors to correct these abuses and to place these gifts in their proper perspective.

Diversity of Gifts

Paul begins this discussion by saying, "Now concerning spiritual *gifts*" (12:1). You will note that "gifts" is in italics, which means that this word is not in the Greek text. Literally, he said, "Now concerning [about] the spirituals" or "the spiritualities" (*tōn pneumatikōn*).[1] G. Campbell Morgan is helpful as to Paul's meaning. Up to this point the apostle has been dealing with the carnalities which were dividing the Corinthian church. Now he turns to the *spiritualities,* including the doctrine of the resurrection (chap. 15), which were also sources of disharmony.

However, Paul quickly centers his attention upon spiritual *gifts* as seen in 12:4: "Now there are diversities of gifts." [2] These were *gifts of grace* bestowed upon various people with no thought of merit on the part of the donee. The word "diversities" means not only differences but distributions. Different gifts were distributed on various people. The words "differences" (v.5) and "diversities" (vv.4,6) all render the same Greek word. So there are diversities of *gifts, administrations* (ministrations or services), and *operations* (performances). But there are "the same Spirit . . . the same Lord . . . the same God" (vv.4–6). Note that all of these gifts are from the Triune God (cf. 1 Cor. 12:28; Eph. 4:11).

Paul speaks of these gifts as a "manifestation of the Spirit" (v.7), the Spirit of God sent forth to do his work. This is another of those instances in which the divine work is attributed to first one and then another, or all, of the persons of the Godhead. But the immediate agent in this bestowal is the Holy Spirit.

These gifts are given for a purpose. They are bestowed "to every man to profit withal" (v.7). Though in some cases these gifts may edify the individual, their primary purpose is to edify the body of believers and to enable it to do the work of the Lord (cf. 6:12; 10:23,33). So no gift of the Holy Spirit is to be used selfishly or for self-glory. Each is to glorify Christ.

Then Paul proceeds to list these gifts:

The word of wisdom (v.8).—This means speech filled with God's wisdom, used under the impulse of the Holy Spirit (cf. 2:7) and the practical action in accord with it. The fact that the apostle lists this gift first suggests that all others are to be exercised within its sphere.

The word of knowledge (*v.8*).—This gift suggests illumination or insight which enables one to comprehend the things of the Spirit.

Faith (*v.9*).—Faith here is not saving faith. Rather it means faith to work wonders (cf. 13:2), or the faith which enables one to be trustworthy to the task to which he is assigned (cf. Heb. 11).

The gifts of healing (*v.9*).—This speaks of the ability to perform miraculous healing.

The working[s] of miracles [*powers*] (*v.10*).—This may or may not involve healing. It refers to any wondrous work for God (cf. Acts 13:8–11).

Prophecy (*v.10*).—Prophecy means not only to foretell but more often to tell forth. It was primarily "a speaking forth of God's message under the guidance of the Holy Spirit." [3] But here it probably means an unusual ability to do so.

Discerning of spirits (*v.10*).—This was the ability to judge between evil spirits and the Holy Spirit (cf. 1 Tim. 4:1 ff.; 1 John 4:1–2.).

Tongues or languages (*v.10*).—There is a difference of opinion as to the meaning of "tongues" in 1 Corinthians. Clearly at Pentecost it was the ability to speak a language other than one's own without having learned it. The interpretation of tongues was the ability to interpret a "tongue" to those present who were not versed in it. Note that "tongues" are placed last.

Later in the chapter Paul repeats some of these gifts, preceding them with certain offices which were bestowed by the Holy Spirit: apostles, prophets, teachers (v.28). In Ephesians 4:11, he lists these, along with "evangelists" and "pastors," as the gifts which the ascended Christ bestowed upon the church or gave to men (Eph. 4:8).[4]

Apostles in this sense probably were those pioneers who opened

up new fields of labor. These included those who had been with
Jesus, plus Paul, Barnabas, and certain others. *Prophets* were those
especially gifted in preaching the gospel. *Evangelists* were bearers
of the good news, but seemed to have been more stationary than
apostles and prophets. Some would liken them to district mis-
sionaries. *Pastors* and *teachers* probably refer to the same office
connected with a given congregation (cf. Acts 20:28). Of course,
others were teachers or those especially gifted in explaining the
Scriptures (cf. Acts 18:26). One person, such as Paul, might in a
sense occupy more or all of these offices.

Paul says that each of these various gifts was given by the
Holy Spirit, and he works or energizes each one separately "even
as he wills" (1 Cor. 12:11). Literally, "All these things work the
one and the same Spirit, dividing to every last man even as he
wills." So there is no basis for personal pride should one possess
either one or all of these gifts. He has only that which the Holy
Spirit has given and works in him. This is an important truth.

Unity in Diversity

In a marvelous figure of human anatomy, Paul shows the importance and function of these spiritual gifts in the body of Christ.
The purpose is that they shall function through *unity in diversity*
(12:12 ff.). As the human body is one but possessing many different members with specific functions, so also is the body of
Christ. If the body, human or spiritual, is to function properly, then
each member must discharge its *gift* in a harmonious relationship
to all other members. Otherwise there is a schism, and the body
becomes a chaos rather than a cosmos. As the Holy Spirit brought
a cosmos out of chaos in nature, so it is his function with respect
to the body of Christ.

Thus in the body of Christ people of diverse racial backgrounds
and social stations (Jew, Gentile, bond, and free) are fused into
one new people by the power of the Holy Spirit (v.13). Paul says,

"By one Spirit are we all baptized into one body . . . and have been all made to drink [were drenched] into [in] one Spirit."

Now to what does "baptized" refer? Findlay sees this as related to Christian baptism: "At their baptism the Corinthian believers, differing in race and rank, were consciously made one; *one* Spirit flooded their souls with the love and joy of a common faith in Christ." [5] Robertson also sees Christian baptism "when each of them put on the outward badge of service to Christ, the symbol of the inward changes already wrought in them by the Holy Spirit (Gal. 3:27; Rom. 6:2 ff.)." [6]

But is this what Paul is saying here? He says, "By [*en,* in the sphere of] one Spirit we all into [*eis*] one body were baptized . . . all in the sphere of one Spirit were drenched." *En* marks the sphere, the Holy Spirit, *eis* denotes the relationship, "into one body." To be sure baptism figures as a symbol in the normal experience of a believer. But we have seen that the coming of the Holy Spirit upon a believer is not necessarily related to Christian baptism (i.e. the house of Cornelius). There is no preconceived pattern by which the Holy Spirit works. John the Baptist said that Jesus would baptize with the Holy Spirit in contrast to water baptism. Jesus also says that the Holy Spirit indwells the believer.

Therefore, may we not say that the baptism to which Paul refers is the baptism of the Holy Spirit? At Pentecost the Spirit came upon the church in Jerusalem, thereby fusing a diverse group into a *koinōnia,* or fellowship, one body. At times and for specific reasons he manifested himself in demonstrable signs throughout Acts in connection with the conversion experience.

But in view of Jesus' word about the indwelling of the Spirit (John 14:17), are we not justified in seeing the more normal coming of the Spirit into the heart the moment one becomes a believer as his being baptized in the sphere of the Holy Spirit? He is *drenched* in the sphere of the Spirit, and thus enters into this new relationship. He becomes a part of the *koinōnia* of the body of

Christ. Failure to realize this causes many Christians, as at Corinth, to fail to recognize this *koinōnia*. They become problem members in the body of Christ rather than helpful ones.

Even in this *fellowship* each member retains his identity, "for the body is not one member, but many" (1 Cor. 12:14). Thus, there always exists the possibility of conflict in personality and in function. When such happens the entire body, including the head (Eph. 4:15), suffers.

The members should not play one gift or function over against another. Simply because one Christian cannot perform as another does not mean that he is not a part of the body (1 Cor. 12:15–16). If all had the same gift the body would not be a cosmos but a monstrosity, such as one big eye or ear (v.17). So, according to his will, the Holy Spirit has distributed these gifts to insure one well-rounded, functioning body (vv.18–20). For this reason no one part of the body should look with disdain upon another.

Each member is necessary for the well-being of all others (vv. 21–22). In the human body the hidden organs are more necessary for life than those that are seen. In fact, without the former the latter would fail entirely. So in the church the *hidden* members working in the background are of greater importance than those who function in the pulpit, choir, or some other more publicized capacity (vv.23–24).

The *body* should shun divisions as each member functions as a unified part of the whole (v.25). Each member should be concerned about the welfare of all others. No part of the body can either suffer or rejoice but that it has a corresponding effect upon all others. If one Christian is shamed or honored, it reflects likewise upon all other Christians—and upon Christ. So while we are members of the body of Christ, we are members in particular. But like some mighty organ, when each part in harmony with all others functions in its own particular sphere, the result is a glorious symphony of praise and service to God (vv.28–30). If this is to be made possible, then each member must lose himself in the *koinōnia* wrought by the Holy Spirit.

Christian Love

"But covet earnestly the best [greater] gifts" (12:31). This shows that Paul ranks some gifts above others. It is of interest to note that these "greater gifts" are not the outward display of the things so often related to the power of the Holy Spirit. In light of the overall, it is possible to list these as faith, hope, love—and, perhaps, prophecy, or the gift of proclaiming the gospel of grace in Spirit-given power.

The apostle says, "Yet shew I unto you a more excellent way" than the selfish display of and dispute over ecstatic gifts (v.31). This is the *huperbolēn hodon,* the above and beyond or "the supremely excellent way."

This introduces us to the *love chapter* (1 Cor. 13), which has been called "Paul's Ode to Love." However, it is hardly conceivable that a master logician like Paul would suddenly break his chain of thought to write a poetic utterance on the theme of love. The truth is that he comes to the climax of his argument as he shows the spirit in which the gifts of the Holy Spirit should be exercised. This is the superlative way of *Christian love.*

Unfortunately, the King James Version renders this word "charity." The Greek word is *agapē,* the kind of love which characterizes the very nature of God (cf. John 3:16; 1 John 4:8 ff.). It is the love which God has for us, which we in Christ express toward him, and which in Christ we should exercise toward other Christians. Hence, *Christian love.* W. Hersey Davis once described this love as being a state of absolute loyalty to the object of one's love. It is this love which should permeate the Christian fellowship.

Paul makes three definite statements about love. First, he

speaks of *the necessity of love* in Christian relationships (vv.1–3). The Corinthian Christians were divided over the relative importance of spiritual gifts such as tongues, prophecy, wisdom and knowledge, faith, miracles or wonders, and deeds of mercy (i.e. healings). But Paul says that if he could speak all the tongues of men, even some known only to angels, and did so apart from Christian love, he would be making just so much noise. It would be nothing more than the crashing sound of the brass gong and the lilting, empty notes of cymbals used in pagan temples of worship (such as the temple of Aphrodite, located on the Acro-Corinthus, eighteen hundred feet above Corinth).

In this negative approach, the priority of tongues makes this gift of least importance (cf. 12:10,28). Even though he could prophesy, know all mysteries and knowledge, and have faith to enable him to work the wonder of moving mountains, unless he did these things in love he would be nothing.

"I am nothing" (13:2) is an emphatic statement. He did not say, "I am nobody [*outheis*]" but "I am no thing [*outhen*]," literally, "Nothing I am" or "I am a zero."

Even philanthropy and martyrdom without Christian love are profitless. "Bestow" (v.3) is an aorist tense, suggesting one grand gift of all of one's possessions. Such could be done out of pity or a desire for credit. One might even surrender his body to a fiery martyr's death, as, indeed, some early Christians did. But if even this is done out of any motive other than Christian love, "it profiteth me nothing." He winds up with nothing—another zero. No goods, no life, no merit. Nothing! So love is the qualifying grace which gives meaning to all of the Christian's deeds.

Second, Paul speaks of the *characteristics of love* (vv.4–7). "Love is longsuffering." It does not lose heart. It is patient in bearing insult or injury without anger or vengeance. Love "is kind" or gentle in conduct. Instead of striking back at its tormentors, it seeks ways of helping them. Love "envieth not." It does not boil with zeal for a wrong cause. Neither does it boil with jealousy over the gifts and accomplishments of others.

It "vaunteth not itself." Neither is it a braggart, nor does it promote its own welfare. "Is not puffed up" with pride, as one blown up by a bellows (cf. 5:2). "Doth not behave itself unseemly." It is not characterized by indecent behavior. "Seeketh not her own"; is not selfish or self-seeking. "Is not easily provoked." Love does not fly off the handle in a paroxysm of anger.

Love "thinketh no evil." This is not a fourth little monkey of Nikko: see no evil, hear no evil, speak no evil, *think no evil.* Literally, "Love does not keep books on the evil done against it." Love does not rejoice in the existence or the triumph of unrighteousness. Rather it rejoices in truth and its victories.

"Beareth all things" means to build a protecting roof over others. "Love covers a multitude of sins" (1 Peter 4:8, RSV), Christ's love and Christian love. Thus love does not disregard the sins of others, but it shows compassion and understanding toward the evildoer.

"Believeth all things" does not mean gullibility but faith in others. "Hopeth" suggests that one looks on the bright side of adversity, expecting righteousness to triumph. To endure all things is to be a stouthearted soldier, taking all that the enemy can throw at you but still having the reserve with which to countercharge to victory.

Third, the apostle speaks of *the enduring nature of love* (1 Cor. 13:8–13). The gift of Christian love will outlast all other spiritual gifts. For they are temporary and temporal gifts; love is eternal.

"Love never fails." It does not "fall" (*piptō*). "Never" renders a strong negative, "never at any time." J. H. Thayer notes that it denies absolutely and objectively, "not ever." As Robertson says, "Love survives everything." [7] "But," in contrast to love, "prophecies . . . *shall fail* . . . knowledge, it *shall vanish away*" (au-

thor's italics). These italicized words render the same Greek verb
which means to render idle or inoperative. The time will come
when these gifts no longer will function. Even prophecy or the
preaching of the gospel will not be needed after the return of the
Lord.

But what about *tongues?* "They shall cease." This is a stronger
statement than that concerning prophecy and knowledge. The tone
of their being rendered inoperative suggests a longer duration.
But tongues shall *cease.* This verb is a middle (reflexive) form.
Robertson says that tongues "shall make themselves cease or
automatically cease of themselves." [8] In all likelihood this gift
ceased with the first century.

At best our knowledge and prophesying are fragmentary or "in
part." But when that which is "perfect" or complete is come, then
these fragmentary things "shall be rendered inoperative" (v.10).
They will have fulfilled their function, like a flower which buds,
blossoms, and then falls away. The "perfect" could refer to the
second coming of Christ. Then our "knowledge" (*gnōsis*) will become "full knowledge" (*epignōsis*), and prophecy will give way to
praise.

Paul illustrates this truth concerning all spiritual gifts, except
love, with the figure of a child (v.11). Five times in this verse
he uses the word *nēpios,* meaning a veritable baby. The thought
here is that of immature Christians. So literally, "When I was a
baby, I used to talk as a *baby,* I used to understand as a *baby,* I
used to reason as a *baby;* when I *became* a man I *rendered
inoperative* the things of the *baby*" (author's italics). "Became"
and "rendered inoperative" are perfect tenses, meaning a permanent thing. He does not act like a baby anymore.

In effect, Paul says that these ecstatic spiritual gifts are like children's toys. These Corinthian Christians are like babies, fussing
over their toys. They should grow up and act like adults. Toys
have their place in a baby's life, but they do not belong in an

adult's life. Toys that will either cease altogether or else will be rendered inoperative are the cause of destroying the *koinōnia* of that church—that is, the abuse of them is doing so. They were given by the Holy Spirit for a purpose, but that purpose did not relate to a nursery.

As if this were not enough, the apostle added another illustration—that of looking in a mirror (v.12). The mirror in question was made of polished metal which gave a blurred image. At best this knowledge was blurred. In heaven, which should be the standard of measure for the Christian's present conduct, we shall see not a blurred image but "face to face." All the things which were troubling them could, through their full surrender to the Holy Spirit, be brought into a clear focus. "Now I know in part; but then shall I know even as also I am known" (v.12). Literally, "I shall fully know as I am fully known." To be sure, this is the heavenly picture. But by exercising Christian love, even on earth the believer can move toward that goal.

In concluding this chapter Paul lists the three Christian virtues—faith, hope, and love (v.13). All three are abiding in quality in contrast to the temporary gifts over which his readers were wrangling. "But the greatest of these is love." It is an attribute of God, and qualifies both faith and hope (cf. vv.2,7).

Here Paul is looking beyond this life to the life beyond. There he implies that even faith and hope will be rendered inoperative. *Faith* will become *sight; hope* will become *realization.* Only *love* will remain. For in eternity we shall go on loving God and being loved by him. It is no wonder, therefore, that this love is the supreme gift of the Holy Spirit.

Prophecy and Proclamation

Having dealt generally with spiritual gifts, Paul now turns to a specific problem. In doing so he nails down the matter of love when he says, "Follow after charity [love]" (14:1), or chase love until you seize upon it. He does not say that they should ignore their *spiritualities,* but they should exercise them in love to the end that each one may be used to prophesy or to proclaim the gospel of Christ.

This brings him to a comparison of the gifts of prophecy and tongues. Quite clearly he values the former above the latter (vv. 2–5). A man speaking in tongues does not speak to men, unless they understand, but to God alone. One who prophesies to men so as to be understood edifies, encourages, and gives incentive toward righteous living and endeavor (v.3).

Tongues may build up the speaker, but preaching edifies the church (v.4). Paul wishes that every Christian had the gift of tongues. But even more, he wishes that they shall preach. Definitely, says he, the latter is to be preferred above the former (v.5).

What are we to understand by "tongues" in Corinth? For the most part New Testament scholars agree that "tongues" at Pentecost were intelligible languages. They were a gift of the Holy Spirit whereby the speakers miraculously were enabled to speak languages and/or dialects other than their own. This was to enable the various groups present to hear the gospel in their own tongues. As Stagg says, "The gift of tongues at Pentecost served Christian missions at a crucial juncture of redemptive history." He is also correct when he says, "It is not clear what was the nature of 'tongues' in the home of Cornelius (Acts 10:46) and in Ephesus (19:6)." [9] But whatever it was it was a genuine evidence of the work of the Holy Spirit.

However, Stagg sees no relationship between the phenomena at Pentecost and Corinth. He recognizes that Paul regarded "tongues" at Corinth as a gift of the Holy Spirit, even though a lesser one. But he also comments, "Modern 'glossolalia' movements confuse Pentecost and Corinth. The ecstatic and unintelligible utterance at Corinth is cloaked with the respectability of Pentecost. Modern tongues are Corinthian, not Pentecostal." [10]

But even if this be true, does this not also clothe this modern "glossolalia" with the respectability of Paul's recognition that "tongues" at Corinth were a gift of the Holy Spirit? So can we justifiably relate the modern "glossolalia" with either Pentecost or Corinth, except that at Corinth "tongues" were a problem in the church even as "glossolalia" is today?

Modern "glossolalia" claims to be an evidence of the "second blessing" or of the presence of the Holy Spirit in one's life. We have noted previously that the New Testament does not teach a "second blessing." So can we rightly say that the present-day phenomenon rests upon New Testament teaching?

With regard to modern "glossolalia," the author finds himself in agreement with an article by Frank W. Beare. The following points are made: The Gospels record no instances of speaking in tongues; it is never attributed to Jesus; it was never promised by Jesus to any of his followers (Mark 16:9–20 not in best manuscripts; cf. v.17b). In the Sermon on the Mount he warned against empty or "vain repetitions" (Matt. 6:7). The Greek verb is a rare one, composed of the verb to speak prefixed by the word "Batta." The word sounds like, "Do not go on saying, 'Batta, batta, batta." Dr. Beare comments, "In the context of the sermon it clearly does not refer to a mere defect in speech but to the repetition of the meaningless sounds (abracadabra). Instead of this heathenish resort to magical formula, they are bidden to say, 'Our Father.' " [11]

In Jesus' great passage on the Holy Spirit he said nothing about speaking in tongues (cf. John 14–16). When he breathed the Holy Spirit on the apostles, *tongues* are not mentioned (John 20:22). There were times in Acts where the Spirit came apart from *tongues*.

Noting that Paul deals with the matter of *tongues* only in 1 Corinthians, Dr. Beare says, "This fact is in itself significant, for he is the great theologian of the Holy Spirit. In Romans . . . there is a rich and varied exposition of the work of the Spirit without the faintest suggestion that it includes any 'speaking with tongues.' " [12]

So then we can conclude that modern "glossolalia" is related neither to Pentecost nor to Corinth. Many scholars relate it to the latter, holding that both are unintelligible utterances spoken in ecstasy. But, as will be seen shortly, the Corinthian "tongues" lend themselves to another explanation. Certainly those who hold to the "unknown tongue" find no support in 1 Corinthians, for the word "unknown" does not appear in the Greek text (cf. 1 Cor. 14:2,4,13–14,19,27).

Some modern adherents to "glossolalia" claim to speak in foreign languages that the speaker has not previously known. Others insist that they speak a heavenly language which can be interpreted only by the Holy Spirit. Certainly the latter cannot be disproved by mere man. But there is reason to question the former. One pastor claims that he spoke in Latin. He even tape-recorded the experience! But he refused to permit a Latin teacher to hear the recording. This sort of experience seems to be more emotional and psychological than spiritual.

Modern "glossolalia" tends to exalt the Holy Spirit beyond any teaching found in the New Testament. Jesus said, "He shall glorify me" (John 16:14). Certainly in this area of theological thought we need to "try the spirits whether they are of God" (1 John 4:1).

Certainly we agree with Trentham when he says that "we are on New Testament ground when we conclude that speaking in tongues is not regarded by any New Testament writer as an invariable accompaniment of the life of grace. Neither does the New

Testament regard a Christian who has not had this experience as inferior to those who have had it." [13]

This still leaves us with the problem at Corinth. What, if any, is the relationship between "tongues" at Pentecost and "tongues" in Corinth? And why is it that only in Corinth was Paul called upon to deal with this matter?

Perhaps we can expedite matters by stating that the author believes that the phenomena at Pentecost and Corinth are one, with one great difference. At Pentecost the gift was used as the Holy Spirit intended. But at Corinth this gift, as all other of the ecstatic gifts, was abused for selfish pride rather than for the furtherance of the gospel. In this sense they were a gift of the Holy Spirit. But, by an evil spirit many who possessed the gift of tongues were led to abuse it. It is even possible that some not possessing the gift were led of an evil spirit to try to imitate it.

Now there are many who hold that "tongues" at Corinth were more of an unintelligible utterance made in spiritual ecstasy. Trentham points out that some of the leaders in the church in Corinth may have been shocked by some things spoken in such a condition. He cites as a possibility the statement "Jesus is accursed" (1 Cor. 12:3). "This spirit would not have been the Spirit of God. Unintelligible utterances may be prompted by an evil spirit." [14]

May not an evil spirit have prompted the abuse of the gift of speaking an intelligible language, at least intelligible to some? "Jesus is accursed" was certainly not unintelligible, as Paul indicates. It is entirely possible that "the prevalence of ecstatic speech among the frenzied priests and priestesses of the Greek oracles (particularly that of Apollo at Delphi, which was not far away) would help account for the high value placed upon it [tongues] by the Corinthians." [15] Even the utterances in the temple of Aphrodite, for that matter. But does this mean that the utterances in the Corinthian church were unintelligible? Is there not some other explanation for Paul's words in 1 Corinthians 14:6 ff.?

The language certainly does not justify a distinction between Pentecost and Corinth. In both cases the word is *glōssa,* tongue. Of course, the basic meaning of the word refers to the tongue as the organ of speech (cf. 14:9).

The next meaning is that of *language* as at Pentecost. One of the best Greek lexicons [16] gives a third meaning as "the broken speech of persons in religious ecstasy." It refers to this phenomenon in Greek pagan religion. Certainly this was true of pagan religions. But does it necessarily follow that we must transfer this pagan meaning to the Christian context in Corinth? If there were no Pentecost example of the word, we would have no hesitancy in agreeing with this position. But since there is, then we should first of all examine the Corinthian situation against that background.

Why do we find this situation only in Corinth? At Pentecost the multilingual group explains "tongues" there. Where else in the Greco-Roman world would one be more likely to find such a condition on a large scale than in Corinth? It was the greatest commercial center in the Roman Empire. People from all parts of the world were drawn together to form a polyglot population.

If there were any one place in that day where the Holy Spirit would have given the gift of tongues as at Pentecost, Corinth would be a primary candidate for such. With merchants and traders from all parts of the world going and coming, it was a glorious opportunity to preach to men of every kindred, tongue, and nation, and through them to spread the gospel wherever they went.

At the same time the Corinthian Christians were very susceptible to the pagan influences and practices about them (cf. 1 Cor. 6:15–18; 10:21). The pagan ecstatic utterances at Delphi and the temple of Aphrodite would prove a snare to those Christians who had the gift of tongues. They would prove to be easy prey to the evil spirit who sought to lead them to use this Spirit-given ability for empty, prideful public display. To confuse further the issue, this evil spirit could have produced a *pseudotongue*. Thus that which was intended to be used to preach to a multilingual city became a scandal to those who could not understand the language being spoken.

Now, in this light, let us examine Paul's words in 1 Corinthians 14. Apparently the major problem at Corinth centered in prophecy and speaking in tongues. Since both of these gifts involved public speaking, there may have been a conflict between these two groups. Therefore, after dealing with the problem surrounding spiritual gifts in general, Paul focused on prophesying and tongues in particular. It is clear that the apostle regards tongues as the lesser of these two gifts (vv.1–4).

In verse 5 he expresses the wish that all might speak in foreign languages. But it is greater to preach in one's own tongue rather than in languages "except one may interpret." Only thus could the church, or those who did not understand the language, be edified.

Suppose, says Paul, he should come to Corinth speaking a language which they did not understand. What profit would it be to them unless he gave them a revelation, or knowledge, or prophecy, or teaching? None of this would be of value unless they understood his words (v.6). Even musical sounds have no meaning unless the hearer understands them. If the trumpet gives an uncertain voice, the soldiers cannot prepare for battle (vv.7–8). Neither of these three examples (vv.6–8) is incompatible with the speaking of a foreign language which is intelligible to someone but not to the hearers.

So Paul says that by their tongue (organ of speech) the Corinthians should speak a language which their hearers could understand. If they spoke Egyptian to a group which understood only Greek, they would simply be speaking into the air (v.9).

That Paul is speaking of intelligible languages is seen in verses 10–11. There are so many kinds of voices or sounds *in the world,* not some heavenly language, "and none of them is without signification," or as Robertson comments, "without the faculty of speech." [17]

These sounds mean something to somebody somewhere. For instance, the clicking of a telegraph device says nothing to an untrained ear, but it speaks intelligently to one who knows the code. "Therefore," says Paul, "if I know not the meaning of the voice, I shall be unto him that speaketh a barbarian, and he that speaketh shall be a barbarian unto me" (v.11). This has a definite reference to intelligible languages.

The Greeks called all who did not understand their language "barbarians." The Greek word *barbaros* has the sound of such a foreign language. A Jew speaking Aramaic to a Greek who did not understand the language sounded to the Greek like "bar bar." But the sound was intelligible to the Jew. So Paul says that speaking in a foreign language could separate rather than unite the speaker and the hearer. Therefore, the apostle says that no one should speak in a foreign tongue unless there is someone present to interpret it to those in the audience who do not understand the language (v.13).

How could one interpret an unintelligible sound? To say that the interpreter only gave the background of the speaker's experience of ecstasy hardly satisfies Paul's language.

With respect to prayer, Paul says that if he prays in a tongue, his "spirit prayeth" but his "understanding is unfruitful" (v.14). Does he mean that his spirit prays but his intellect does not know what he is praying? Some raise the question as to whether "tongues" at Pentecost constituted a miracle of speaking or of hearing. If this be only a miracle of hearing, this could be the meaning here—that even the one speaking in a tongue did not know what he was saying.

We believe that the miracle was both speaking and hearing. To be exact, the speaker spoke a foreign tongue and the one whose tongue it was heard it. Thus, in essence, it was a miracle of speaking. A possible meaning is that Paul says that if those who hear him pray do not understand his words, his intellect is unfruitful for them. It bears no fruit that they can understand. So Paul concludes that both prayer and singing should be both emotional for him and intelligent to those who hear (v.15).

This position seems to be supported by verses 16–17. Even if at the Lord's Supper one blesses or prays in a foreign language, how shall those who are "unlearned" in that language even say "amen" at the proper place? Robertson notes that in the synagogues the Jews gave responsive *amens* at the close of prayers. Everyone who has heard another pray in a foreign tongue knows of this problem. One may give thanks well (*kalōs*), or pray beautifully, but if it is in a language not understood by the hearers it does not edify them (v.17).

Paul gives his own evaluation of speaking in languages (vv. 18–19). He excels all others in this. But in the church he would rather speak five words intelligently than ten thousand in a tongue which was not understood. His citing of Isaiah 28:11 shows that the matter under discussion involves languages intelligible to someone (v.21).

Now what is the purpose of the ability to speak in foreign tongues? They are a "sign," not to those who already believe. It seems that they would be if they were nothing more than some utterance in spiritual ecstasy, or a sign of the speaker's spiritual excellence. But they are a sign to unbelievers. The ability for a Jew to speak of Christ to an unbelieving African who spoke some language other than the speaker's own would be a "sign" (*sēmeion*) to the African that God was in the speaking. Contrariwise, prophesying in plain language is for the believers, not the nonbelievers who do not understand it.

However, caution must be exercised in the use of tongues (v. 23). Suppose that the entire church were assembled, and everyone was speaking in tongues. Assuming that each one spoke a different language, the result would be bedlam. This situation presupposes that everyone was exercising his gift for no purpose other than self-glory, since apparently there was none present to whom tongues would be necessary to witness.

Paul deliberately reduces this abuse of languages to the absurd. In such a case, an uninstructed unbeliever would think that he was in a madhouse. On the other hand, if in a similar situation all were preaching in a language that the unbeliever understood, he would be convicted of his sin and be saved (vv.24–25). So Paul says that whatever is done should be done, not for personal glory, but for the building up of the church (v.26).

If the use of gifts is to result in edification instead of bedlam, then they must be exercised in an orderly fashion. So Paul centers on the two greatest problems, tongues and prophecy, and sets forth regulations by which they shall be expressed.

Not everyone capable of speaking in tongues should do so at one time (vv.27–28; cf. v.23). Only two, or at most three, should speak in a given service. And that "by course" or in turn, each taking his turn. One should interpret, so that those not understanding the language spoken might understand. But if there should be no interpreter present, then the tongue speaker should keep silent (v.28). His communion should be between himself and God. This does not within itself mean that a tongue was only a spiritual ecstasy. The tone of the language implies an intelligible utterance capable of being interpreted.

Likewise, *ground rules* were laid down for prophesying. Only two or three should speak at a given service (v.29; cf. v.24), and that one by one (v.31). The other prophets present should discern whether the thing proclaimed was of the Holy Spirit or of an evil spirit (cf. 12:10; 1 John 4:1). No one prophet was to speak too long. And if a silent prophet signified, probably by a gesture, that he had received a revelation, the speaker should sit down and let the other speak.

This would not be a bad rule to follow today. If one speaker has run out of something to say, would it not be well for him to give place to one who does have a message? It might embarrass the one brother, but it would edify the church. A very fine definition of preaching is to have something to say, say it, and sit down.

Furthermore, "the spirits of the prophets are subject to the prophets" (v.32). This presupposes some prophet's objecting to being asked to sit down right in the middle of his message. He could not turn prophecy on and off as by a switch. But Paul says that the possessor of this gift should be able to control his use of it.

G. G. Findlay remarks, "This Divine gift is put under the control and responsibility of the possessor's will, that it may be exercised with discretion and brotherly love, for its appointed ends. An unruly prophet is therefore no genuine prophet; he lacks one of the necessary marks of the Holy Spirit's indwelling." [18] For God is not characterized by confusion, but of peace. Worship in the churches, therefore, should be orderly (v.33).

Paul has a special word for women in the Corinthian church (vv.34–35). Already he has dealt with their abuse of dress (11: 2–16). It appears that they also were creating a problem as to public speech. Some, even without the gift, may have been posing as speaking in tongues or else as prophesying. So he tells them to "keep silence in the church" (cf. vv.28,30).

Some see this as a general injunction against women speaking in church. However, the daughters of Philip were prophetesses (Acts 21:9). In all likelihood Paul was dealing with a specific case. In many pagan temples such as the one of Aphrodite, priestesses, who were actually immoral women, chanted in ecstasies. Christian women prophesying or speaking in tongues could be mistaken by the pagans as similar to their priestesses. So they should not speak in the churches, but should inquire of their husbands at home as to matters of their concern.

Paul concludes his treatment of gifts of the Holy Spirit by saying that the Corinthian Christians should not forbid anyone to speak in tongues who possessed the gift. But in a stronger word he says that they should be zealous to prophesy, for this is the greater gift (v.39).

But whatever they did in exercising spiritual gifts, it should be done with decorum and discipline. For such will enhance the usefulness of the gift, and will serve to glorify Christ. This is the purpose of the Holy Spirit in conferring these gifts upon men.

Teacher, Guide, and Helper
10

The ideal for the life of a Christian is one that is lived in the atmosphere of the Holy Spirit. Anything short of this is to miss the mark of God's will for his people. Indeed, it is impossible for a Christian to divorce himself from the presence of the Holy Spirit. Yet, there is tragic evidence on every hand of indifferent, fruitless Christian lives. Spiritual infants abound on every hand.

Far too many Christians are described in the words of Hebrews 5:12–14: "For when for the time ye ought to be teachers, ye have need that one teach you again which be the first principles of the oracles of God, and are become such as have need of milk, and not of strong meat. For every one that useth milk is unskilful in the word of righteousness: for he is a babe. But strong meat belongeth to them that are of full age [adults], even those who by reason of use have their senses exercised to discern both good and evil."

With the Holy Spirit available as teacher, guide, and helper, the scandal of our age is those Christians who are as "children, tossed to and fro, and carried about with every wind of doctrine, by the sleight of men, and cunning craftiness, whereby they lie in wait to deceive" (Eph. 4:14). Too many Christians are not "speaking the truth in love"; they are not growing "up into him in all things, which is the head, even Christ" (v.15).

For this reason we conclude this study by noting the Holy

Spirit in the life of the believer. All that has been said previously
will have little practical import unless we fully realize this truth in
experience.

Body of Believers

In Ephesians 5, Paul exhorts his readers to walk in the light,
for "the fruit of the Spirit is in all goodness and righteousness and
truth" (v.9). Then he contrasts the works of darkness and light
by saying, "Be not drunk with wine, wherein is excess [riot]; but
be filled with the Spirit" (v.18). So instead of getting the
temporary *lift* provided by wine, the Christian should have the
abiding exhilaration and glow of personality which comes from
the controlling presence of the Holy Spirit in his life.

Does this command to be filled with the Holy Spirit involve a
"second blessing" or a special infilling by the Spirit? This can
hardly be the case if it be considered in the light of the overall
teachings of the New Testament. Jesus said that the world cannot
receive the Spirit because it neither sees nor knows him. But the
Christian knows him, "for he dwelleth with you, and shall be in
you" (John 14:17).

Thus the Holy Spirit *keeps on dwelling* in the Christian. In
other words, as we have noted previously, at the moment one
believes in Christ the Holy Spirit indwells him, seals him unto God,
and becomes God's *guarantee* or earnest money that God will
go through with his promise to save him completely. Furthermore,
the phenomena in Acts, other than at Pentecost, involve the various manifestations of the Spirit in connection with the conversion
experience.

Even the coming of the Spirit at Pentecost was not the result of
anything that the Christians did. It was in answer to Jesus' prayer
to the Father (John 14:16). The Spirit came in power, and there
is no record that he has since been taken away. Instead, as Paul
says in 1 Corinthians, both the body of the Christian and the body

of believers is the temple, or dwelling place of the Holy Spirit (3:16; 6:19). The present tenses in these verses speak of a continuous effect. The body of the Christian *keeps on being* the temple of the Holy Spirit, which as a group they *keep on having* from God (6:19). And he *keeps on dwelling* in the fellowship of believers (3:16).

However, we must distinguish between the *presence* of the Spirit and the *power* of the Spirit. He is present in power, but the power must become operative in the one whom the Spirit indwells. Jesus promised that the apostles would receive power when the Spirit came upon them (Acts 1:8). But shortly before this he had told them to tarry in Jerusalem "until ye be endued [get yourselves clothed] with power from on high" (Luke 24:49). So there is a difference between the coming of the Spirit and their being clothed with his power.

His coming involved an act of God; getting themselves clothed with his power involved their own acts. We may well imagine that the time between Jesus' ascension and Pentecost was spent by this little Christian group in getting themselves ready to be clothed with the power when the Holy Spirit came in power.

It is in this light that we may understand Paul's command in Ephesians 5:18 ("be filled" is an imperative). Jesus *prayed* the Father, and the Spirit came. Paul *commands* the Christians to be filled with the Spirit. It is not enough to say that the Spirit is here, but not in the Christian, for he indwells the believer arbitrarily without regard to the Christian's will or conduct. We have noted that even those guilty of *unsaintly* conduct are called "saints." This is because the Holy Spirit indwells their spirits, dedicating them to the service of God. But whether or not that arbitrary dedication shall become willing service depends upon the will of the individual "saint."

Therefore, does not Paul's language mean that the Christian should submit himself to the will and direction of the Holy Spirit?

In a sense, he should be *available* for the operation of the Spirit's power in and through his life. Thus being filled with the Spirit does not mean a "second blessing" in which he comes into the life in a special way. It is rather a *dedication* of self. Sin no longer reigns. One yields his body and its powers "unto God, as those that are alive from the dead, and your members as instruments of righteousness unto God" (Rom. 6:12–13).

"Present your bodies a living sacrifice, holy, acceptable unto God, which is your reasonable [spiritual] service" (Rom. 12:1). Paul puts it even more strongly in 1 Corinthians 6:19–20: "Know ye not that your body is the temple of the Holy Ghost [Spirit], which is in you, which ye have of God, and ye are not your own? For ye are bought with a price: therefore glorify [imperative] God in your body."

Now this does not imply sinless perfection. The New Testament does not promise such a state in this earthly life. This certainly is no excuse for living a life of sin (cf. Rom. 6:1–2). But the New Testament does recognize that so long as the Christian is in the flesh he is subject to temptation and to yielding to it.

Certain passages in 1 John, written to Christian people, are often cited as teaching sinless perfection. In the King James Version one might make a case for such. But not so in the Greek text. It is impossible to translate into smooth English the finer points of the Greek verb tenses. For instance, the present tense expresses continuous action, to keep on doing or to have the habit of doing something. The aorist tense denotes point action or action at any given point in time. The perfect tense expresses the idea of a finished work. This last is seen in 1 John 1:10: "If we say that we have not sinned [not at any time sinned or will ever sin], we make him a liar, and his word is not in us."

The present tense throws abundant light on other passages. "If we say that we have fellowship with him, and walk [have the habit of walking] in darkness, we lie, and do not the truth: But if we walk [have the habit of walking] in the light, as he is in the light, we have fellowship [*koinōnian*] one with another, and the blood of Jesus Christ his Son cleanseth [keeps on cleansing] us from all sin" (vv.6–7). Sinless perfection is clearly denied in verse 8: "If we say that we have [keep on having] no sin, we deceive ourselves, and the truth is not in us."

Still further, "Whosoever abideth [has the habit of abiding] in him sinneth not [does not have the habit of sinning]: whosoever sinneth [the one having the habit of sinning] hath not seen [perfect] him" (3:6). The perfect tenses show that a person who makes sin the habit or very purpose of his life has never at any time either seen or known the Lord. For "he that committeth [has the habit of doing] sin is of the devil; . . . whosoever is born [perfect, a finished work] of God doth not commit sin [does not have the habit of doing sin]; for his [God's] seed remaineth [keeps on abiding] in him: and he cannot sin [does not have the power to keep on sinning or having the habit of sinning], because he is born [perfect, finished work] of God" (vv.8–9).

To climax the whole, note 1 John 1:9 and 2:1. Literally, "If we keep on confessing our sins, he keeps on being faithful and just, in order that he may *forgive* us our sins, and may *cleanse* us from all unrighteousness" (1:9). The italicized words are aorist tenses of point action. He forgives and cleanses at every point of true, repentant confession. "My little children [a Christian term], these things I write to you in order that you may not at any time sin [aorist, or may immediately stop sinning]. And if anyone may at any time sin [aorist], we keep on having [present] a Paraclete [helper] face to face with the Father" (2:1).

Now the substance of all this is quite plain. The fact that salvation is by grace is no excuse for continuing to live in sin. Indeed, one who has the habit of sinning, or who lives for that very purpose, has never known the grace of God unto salvation. However, the Christian is not promised sinless perfection in this life. He may at times succumb to temptation and fall into sin. But he will repent and confess his sin.

At each given point of confession God forgives. Man has a helper who is ever face to face with God on his behalf. This is the very point of sanctification. At the moment of the new birth the Christian is sanctified, or set apart, to God's service. But he must grow in that state of sanctification.

Implied here is a struggle between the flesh and the Spirit. Progressively, by the power of the Holy Spirit, who indwells him, the Christian wins the victory over sin and yields himself for spiritual service.

Conflict Between the Flesh and the Spirit

"The flesh lusteth against the Spirit, and the Spirit against the flesh: and these are contrary one to the other: so that ye cannot do the things that ye would. But if ye be led of the Spirit, ye are not under the law" (Gal. 5:17–18).

Paul lists the works of the flesh, stating that "they which do [present, having the habit of doing so] such things shall not inherit the kingdom of God" (vv.19–21). This does not mean that the Christian, on occasion, will not be guilty of one or more of these. But they will not be the habit or purpose of his life. However, he can expect his life to be a civil battleground as his flesh wars against his spirit or the Spirit who labors in him to develop him into the likeness of Christ.

Paul describes such a civil war in his own life (Rom. 7:14–25). Some see this as the struggle which raged in him before he became a Christian. But others see implied here the struggle which continued to rage in his life after the Holy Spirit indwelt him. The prevalence of the present tense suggests that the struggle was going on even as he wrote.

In Romans 6:1 to 7:13, Paul is challenging the Christians of

Rome not to yield their bodies to the power of sin but to surrender them to the power of God. Then he cites his own experience to show that such is not an easy thing. He points out that the law of God is spiritual, that which in his law (Ten Commandments) God requires of his people. It is inspired of the Spirit and pertains to the things of the Spirit.

Paul himself is carnal; he is still in the flesh and subject to the weaknesses of the flesh (7:14). As a Christian, he wants to obey God's law, but his carnal self is in rebellion against it. Perhaps a literal translation of a portion of this passage will help us to see this struggle in Paul's life.

For what I am doing I do not know: for not what I am willing, that am I practicing; but what I am hating that am I doing. But if what I am not willing, that I am doing, I am giving consent to the law that it is good. But now no more am I [his true self] doing it, but the sin dwelling in me. [This is no basis for saying that the body sins but the soul does not. Paul is quite clear that you cannot so separate the two.] For I know that there does not dwell in me, that is, in my flesh, good: for to will is always present in me, but not to do constantly [present] the good. For good which I am willing, I am not doing, but evil which I am not willing, that I am doing. But if that which I am not willing, that I am doing, no more I am working it, but the sin dwelling in me. I find then the law, the one in me willing to do the good, that in me the evil is present. For I delight in the law of God after the inward man, but I see a law of a different kind in my members, warring against the law of my mind [spiritual self], and bringing me into captivity in the law of sin which is in my members (vv.15–23).

So Paul finds a conflict in his life between his spiritual self or the mind and his carnal self or the body. In the former he wills or wishes to live according to God's will. But in the latter he finds that he is failing to do so. Instead, he does what his spirit hates and does not do what it wills. He recognizes the power of sin in his body but does not thereby excuse in his spiritual self his sinful acts. Even his true self is captured by the law of sin which indwells the members of his body. But he does not willingly submit to it.

It is no wonder, therefore, that he cries, "O wretched [miserable] man that I am! who shall deliver me from the body of this death?" (v.24). Paul feels that he is imprisoned in a dead body. He has died to sin, but this dead body still holds his living spirit captive. His only consolation is that he belongs to Christ. "I thank God through Jesus Christ our Lord" (v.25). While the struggle goes on, he knows that "I myself with the mind am a slave to the law of God, but with the flesh, the law of sin" (v.25).

In the meantime, what is the Christian's hope? There is no condemnatory judgment to those who are in Christ, for the law of the indwelling Spirit in Christ Jesus has liberated them from the law of sin and death (cf. 8:1–2). Since the law was unable to liberate man through the flesh, God sent his Son in the likeness of sinful flesh. In his Son God condemned sin in the flesh, so that the requirement of the law might be fulfilled in those in Christ, those who walk not after the flesh but after the Spirit (vv.3–4).

"If Christ is in you, the body is dead because of sin; but the spirit [the redeemed human spirit] is life because of righteousness. But if the Spirit of him that raised up Jesus from the dead dwelleth in you, he that raised up Christ Jesus from the dead shall give life also to your mortal bodies through his Spirit that dwelleth in you" (8:10–11, ASV).

Thus the indwelling Spirit not only enables us to overcome the sins of the flesh but in the resurrection will replace our flesh controlled bodies with Spirit controlled bodies (cf. 1 Cor. 15:35–58).

However, before turning from this consideration of the struggle between the flesh and the spirit, we must examine another of Paul's words. First Corinthians 2:14 to 3:23 speaks of three kinds of men: natural, spiritual, and carnal. In each instance the word refers to the principle which controls the man.

The "natural" man is the *psuchikos* man, or one who is controlled by the *psuchē,* the animal principle of life. He is an unregenerate man who lives at the animal level and is controlled by animal instincts and desires, giving no thought to the things of the spirit. The "spiritual" man is the regenerated man. He is the *pneumatikos* man, or the Christian who is controlled by the Holy Spirit. The "carnal" man is a regenerated man, but he is a *sarkikos* man, or a Christian who is controlled by the flesh.

The *natural* man may be likened to a man with self on the throne of his life and Christ on a cross. The *spiritual* man is one who has completely enthroned Christ in his life, with self sitting in submission at the foot of the throne. The *carnal* man is one who tries to place both Christ and self on the throne of his life.

Now Paul says that "the natural man receiveth not the things of the Spirit of God: for they are foolishness unto him: neither can he know them, because they are spiritually discerned" (1 Cor. 2:14; cf. John 14:17). He has had no dealings with either Christ or the Holy Spirit. Therefore, the whole thing is to him moronic. This is a tragedy to be sure. But the tragedy is compounded by the *carnal* Christians all about him. Because of the dual life of such, the natural man is encouraged to remain in his state, even looking with contempt upon God and his way because of them (cf. Rom. 2:24).

Paul describes the Corinthian Christians as "carnal." They were regenerated by the Spirit of God, but they were enslaved by their environment. Therefore, Paul says that he could not speak unto them "as unto spiritual, but as unto carnal, even as unto babes in Christ" (1 Cor. 3:1; cf. Heb. 5:12 ff.). This church was Paul's "problem church." A reading of this epistle reveals how true this is. Not only the sins of the flesh (5:1 ff.; 6:15 f.; 11:21) but the sins of the spirit abounded among them. He cites this latter carnality as evidenced by "envying . . . strife . . .

divisions" (1 Cor. 3:3). This shows that one does not have to be guilty of the more fleshly sins to be a carnal Christian.

Sadly there is an abundance of such among us today. But the greater number of us fall victims to the so-called sins of the spirit. Most Christians flee from fleshly sins as from the devil himself. But alas, multitudes, even preachers, who overcome the blatant fleshly sins fall victims to subtler sins—pride, captious criticism, an unforgiving spirit, and indolence. Many are so absorbed in doing *good* things which have no real spiritual value that they have no time for the more vital matters of time and eternity. We shall continue to be carnal Christians so long as we permit the *good* to become the enemies of the *best*.

Every Christian's life is founded in Christ. But each must build upon that foundation. Too many are building out of "wood, hay, stubble" when they should be using "gold, silver, precious stones" (1 Cor. 3:10–12). The judgment day will declare that out of which each has built (v.13). Many souls will be saved, but their works will not endure (v.15). Why? Because they chose to be carnal rather than spiritual.

Insofar as the individual is concerned, the work of the Holy Spirit may be summed up in two statements—to bring the natural man to become a follower or a "saint" of Christ and to enable such a one to become a fruit-bearing Christian. For in his own life he will have realized the fruit of the Holy Spirit.

Fruit of the Spirit

There is no more beautiful description of the Christian life than that found in Galatians 5:22–23. Here the apostle lists the "fruit of the Spirit" (note the singular). It is that fruit that is borne in the life of the Spirit-controlled Christian. Someone has called this verse a beautiful cluster of luscious grapes—one cluster, which is the fruit of the Spirit, expressing itself in many grapes.

One cannot help but contrast this "fruit" with the outward

signs which some stress as evidence of the presence of the Holy
Spirit in one's life. The quiet, gradual working of the Spirit pro-
duces [1] the fruit—first the leaf, then the bud, then the immature
grape, and finally the ripened grape. There is no sudden coming
of the Spirit with outward signs. Wick Broomall has expressed it
beautifully: "Now as the sap in plant life brings forth fruit in due
season, so the Holy Spirit who indwells believers brings forth a
spiritual harvest." [2]

"But the fruit of the Spirit is love, joy, peace, longsuffering,
gentleness, goodness, faith, meekness, temperance." The "but"
contrasts this fruit with the works of the flesh: "sexual immorality,
impurity, sensuality, idolatry, sorcery, enmity, quarreling, jealousy, anger, intrigues, dissensions, party-spirit, envy, drunken-
ness, carousing, and the like" (Gal. 5:19–21, Williams). These
were all pagan vices. It takes no argument to show that these have
no compatibility with the Christian profession. The fruit of the
Spirit stands out all the more gloriously against such a dark background.

Love, which is the very nature of God, a state of absolute
loyalty to the object of one's love, should characterize every act
of the Christian.

Joy, the exhilarating quality of grace and beauty gives zest
and sparkle to all of life.

Peace, the condition of composure and serenity even in the
midst of a storm, is conditioned not upon outward circumstances
but upon a faith firmly fixed in God and his will.

Longsuffering, the patient endurance of wrongs suffered at the
hand of another, does not stoop to retaliation.

Gentleness, or kindness, seeks to do good to those who have
wronged you.

Goodness, is the quality of uprightness which extends itself to
benefit others in generosity, such as the goodness of God.

Faith, or faithfulness, is the state of trustworthiness and dependability in all of life's relationships.

Meekness, or humility, is courtesy and considerateness in one's dealings with others.

Temperance is self-control and chastity in all of one's physical appetites.

Robertson notes that "Paul has a better list than the four cardinal virtues of the Stoics (temperance, prudence, fortitude, justice), though they are included with better notes struck. Temperance is alike, but kindness is better than justice, long-suffering than fortitude, love than prudence." [3]

This is the cluster of fruit which the Holy Spirit longs to produce in the life of every believer. What a different world this would be were there an abundant harvest of such. Yea, even one such cluster will make life richer and more beautiful for the bearer and for those about him. It will be as turning on one light in the darkness. And when those who walk in darkness see it, they will be drawn to him who is the Light of the world.

Such fruit will not be borne in a day. It is the harvest of a lifetime of yielding to the life of the indwelling Spirit. It is to go on growing in grace and in the knowledge of the Lord Jesus Christ. It is to be constantly moving toward that goal of perfection which is the character of the Heavenly Father. It is to be transformed under the power of the Holy Spirit into the likeness of him in whose face shines the light of the knowledge of the glory of God.

We must begin to form this fruit sometime, somewhere, so why not here—and now?

"If we live in the Spirit, let us also walk in the Spirit" (Gal. 5:25).

NOTES

Chapter 1

1. G. Henton Davies, "The Holy Spirit in the Old Testament," *Review and Expositor*, LXIII (Spring, 1966), 129.

2. *The International Standard Bible Encyclopaedia* (Grand Rapids: Wm. B. Eerdmans Publishing Co., 1949), III, 1407.

3. E. Y. Mullins, *The Christian Religion in Its Doctrinal Expression* (Nashville: Sunday School Board of the Southern Baptist Convention, 1917), pp. 223 ff.

4. *Ibid.,* pp. 206 ff.

Chapter 2

1. A. B. Davidson, *The Theology of the Old Testament* (New York: Charles Scribner's Sons, 1931), p. 121.

2. *Ibid.,* p. 122.

3. *Ibid.*

4. *International Standard Bible Encyclopaedia,* III, 1407.

5. Davies, *op. cit.,* 131.

Chapter 3

1. *International Standard Bible Encyclopaedia,* III, 1410.

2. Frank Stagg, "The Holy Spirit in the New Testament," *Review and Expositor, op. cit.,* 135.

3. *International Standard Bible Encyclopaedia,* III, 1411.

4. Herschel H. Hobbs, *An Exposition of the Gospel of Matthew* (Grand Rapids: Baker Book House, 1965), pp. 43 ff.

5. W. Hersey Davis, *Davis' Notes on Matthew* (Nashville: Broadman Press, 1962), p. 39.

6. *International Standard Bible Encyclopaedia,* III, 1412.

Chapter 4

1. Frank Stagg, *The Book of Acts* (Nashville: Broadman Press, 1955), pp. 4 ff.

2. G. Campbell Morgan, *The Acts of the Apostles* (New York: Fleming H. Revell Co., 1924), p. 24.

3. Stagg, *The Book of Acts,* p. 53.

4. F. J. Foakes-Jackson, *The Acts of the Apostles* ("The Moffatt New Testament Commentary" [New York: Richard R. Smith, 1931]), p. 11.

5. A. T. Robertson, *Word Pictures in the New Testament* (Nashville: Baptist Sunday School Board, 1930), III, 22.

6. For a discussion of "tongues" at Corinth, see chapter 9.

7. Stagg, *The Book of Acts,* p. 83.

8. For a detailed study of this, see chapter 9.

9. Morgan, *op. cit.,* p. 206.

10. *International Standard Bible Encyclopaedia,* III, 1416.

11. For a detailed discussion of this, see chapter 9.

Chapter 5

1. "The Baptist Faith and Message," a statement adopted by the Southern Baptist Convention, 1963.

2. Frank Stagg, *New Testament Theology* (Nashville: Broadman Press, 1962), p. 5.

3. Mullins, *The Christian Religion in Its Doctrinal Expression,* p. 144.

4. Robertson, *op. cit.*

5. *Ibid.*

6. *The Expositor's Greek Testament,* ed. W. Robertson Nicoll

(Grand Rapids: Wm. B. Eerdmans Publishing Co., 1951), V, *in loco.*

Chapter 6

1. *The Expositor's Greek Testament,* I, 824.
2. *International Standard Bible Encyclopaedia,* IV, 2245.
3. Herschel H. Hobbs, *Preaching Values from the Papyri* (Grand Rapids: Baker Book House, 1964), pp. 84 ff.
4. *Word Pictures, op. cit.*
5. *The Expositor's Greek Testament,* I, 836.

Chapter 7

1. "The Baptist Faith and Message," p. 11.
2. *The Expositor's Greek Testament,* I, 835.

Chapter 8

1. Cf. Stagg, *The Book of Acts,* pp. 4 ff.
2. *Ibid.,* pp. 106 ff.
3. Cf. Stagg, *New Testament Theology,* pp. 262 ff.

Chapter 9

1. G. Campbell Morgan, *The Corinthian Letters of Paul* (New York: Fleming H. Revell Co., 1946), pp. 144 ff.
2. Cf. Herschel H. Hobbs, *The Corinthian Epistles* (Grand Rapids: Baker Book House, 1960), pp. 58 ff.
3. Robertson, *op. cit.*
4. Cf. Ray Summers, *Ephesians: Pattern for Christian Living* (Nashville: Broadman Press, 1960), pp. 84–85.
5. *The Expositor's Greek Testament, op. cit.*
6. Robertson, *op. cit.*
7. *Ibid.*
8. *Ibid.*

9. Stagg, "The Holy Spirit in the New Testament," *op. cit.,* 145. "Glossolalia" means speaking in tongues, from the Greek words *glōssa* (tongue) and *lalia* (speaking).

10. *Ibid.*

11. Quoted in Charles A. Trentham, "The New Testament Teaching Concerning Speaking in Tongues," *Journal of Biblical Literature* (September, 1964).

12. *Ibid.*

13. *Ibid.*

14. *Ibid.*

15. *Ibid.*

16. W. F. Arndt and F. W. Gingrich, *A Greek-English Lexicon of the New Testament* (Chicago: University of Chicago Press, 1957).

17. Robertson, *op. cit.*

18. *The Expositor's Greek Testament,* I, 913.

Chapter 10

1. Charles B. Williams, *The New Testament* (Chicago: Moody Press, 1949), renders "fruit" as "product."

2. Wick Broomall, *The Holy Spirit* (New York: American Tract Society, 1940), pp. 181–82.

3. Robertson, *op. cit.*

About the Author

Herschel H. Hobbs has been pastor of the First Baptist Church of Oklahoma City, Oklahoma, since 1949.

He served as president of the Southern Baptist Convention for two years (1962–63). He has been a pastor in Alabama, Indiana, Louisiana, Kentucky, and Oklahoma, also serving on the Foreign Mission Board and as a trustee of New Orleans Baptist Seminary, in addition to other places of denominational service.

A native of Alabama, he received his A.B. degree from Howard College (now Samford University), Birmingham. In addition, he has been awarded the following degrees: Th.M and Ph.D. from Southern Baptist Theological Seminary, Louisville, Kentucky; D.D. from Howard College, and the Litt.D. from William Jewell College, Liberty, Missouri.

For several years Dr. Hobbs has been the nationally-known "Baptist Hour" speaker over more than 500 radio and television stations.

He is the author of several books, including *What Baptists Believe* and *Fundamentals of Our Faith,* also published by Broadman Press.